3

Show What You Know®
FLORIDA!
Preparation for Florida's State Assessment

**Aligned with Florida's
Next Generation
Sunshine State Standards**

Name: _____

Published by:

Show What You Know® Publishing
A Division of Englefield & Associates, Inc.
P.O. Box 341348
Columbus, OH 43234-1348
Phone: 1-877-PASSING (727-7464)
www.showwhatyouknowpublishing.com

Florida Item Distribution information was obtained from the Florida Department of Education Web site, September 2010.

Printed in the United States of America
12 11   20 19 18 17 16 15 14 13 12 11 10 9 8 7 6 5

ISBN: 1-59230-446-X

Show What You Know® Publishing acknowledges the following for their efforts in making this assessment material available for Florida students, parents, and teachers.

Cindi Englefield, President/Publisher
Eloise Boehm-Sasala, Vice President/Managing Editor
Jill Borish, Production Editor
Jennifer Harney, Editor/Illustrator

About the Contributors

The content of this book was written BY teachers FOR teachers and students and was designed specifically for Florida's state assessment for Grade 3 Reading and Mathematics. Contributions to the Reading and Mathematics sections of this book were also made by the educational publishing staff at Show What You Know® Publishing. Dr. Jolie S. Brams, a clinical child and family psychologist, is the contributing author of the Worry Less About Tests and Test-Taking Hints for Test Heroes chapters of this book. Without the contributions of these people, this book would not be possible.

Table of Contents

Introduction

Dear Student:

This *Show What You Know® Florida!, Grade 3 Student Workbook* was created to give you practice for Florida's state assessment in Reading and Mathematics.

The first two chapters in this workbook—Worry Less About Tests and Test-Taking Hints for Test Heroes—were written especially for third-grade students. Worry Less About Tests offers advice on how to overcome nervous feelings you may have about tests.

The Test-Taking Hints for Test Heroes chapter includes helpful tips on how to answer questions correctly so you can succeed on Florida's state assessment.

The next two chapters of this Student Workbook will help you prepare for the Reading and Mathematics assessment.

- The Reading chapter includes a Reading Practice Tutorial, a full-length Reading Assessment, and a Glossary of Reading Terms that will help you show what you know on Florida's state assessment.

- The Mathematics chapter includes a Mathematics Practice Tutorial, a full-length Mathematics Assessment, a Glossary of Mathematics Terms, and a Glossary of Mathematics Illustrations that will help you show what you know on Florida's state assessment.

This Student Workbook will help you become familiar with the look and feel of Florida's state assessment and will provide you with a chance to practice your test-taking skills so you can show what you know.

Good luck on Florida's state assessment!

This page left intentionally blank.

Worry Less About Tests

Introduction

Many of us get nervous or anxious before taking a test. We want to do our best, and we worry that we might fail. Most third graders have probably heard of Florida's state assessment, although they may not be familiar with the actual testing situation. Because Florida's state assessment is new to you, you may become scared. You may worry about the test, and this might interfere with your ability to show what you know.

This chapter offers several tips students can use when they face Florida's state assessment as well as many other tests. The ideas will build confidence.

Worry Less About Tests

There are many things most of us would rather do than take a test. What would you rather do? Go to recess? See a movie? Eat a snack? Go swimming? Take a test? Most of us would not choose take a test. This doesn't mean we're afraid of tests. It means we like to do things that are more fun!

Some students do not want to take tests for another reason. They are afraid of tests and are afraid of failing. Even though they are smart enough to do well, they are scared. All of us worry about a test at one time or another. So, if you worry about tests, you are not alone.

When people worry about tests or are scared of tests, they have what is called test stress. You may have heard your parents say, "I'm feeling really stressed today." That means they have worried feelings. These feelings of stress can get in the way of doing your best. When you have test stress, it will be harder to show what you know. This chapter will help you get over your stress and worry less. You won't be scared. You will feel calm, happy, and proud.

If your mind is a mess
Because of terrible stress,
And you feel that you can't change at all.
Just pick up this book,
And take a look,
Our tips won't let you fall!

It's OK to Worry a Little Bit

Most people worry a little bit about something. Worrying isn't always a bad thing. A small amount of worrying is helpful. If you worry about crossing the street, you are more careful. When you worry about your school work, you work hard to do it right. As you can see, a little worrying isn't bad. However, you have to make sure you don't let worrying get in the way of doing your best. Think about crossing the street. If you worry too much, you'll never go anywhere. You can see how worrying too much is not a good thing.

Third graders have a very special job. That job is taking Florida's state assessment. The people who give Florida's state assessment want to know what you're learning in school.

       © Englefield & Associates, Inc.

What Kind of Kid Are You?

Test stress and worrying too much or too little can get in our way. The good news is there are ways we can help ourselves do better on tests. All we have to do is change the way we think about taking tests. You can do better, not by learning more or studying more, but by changing the way you think about things.

Now you will read about some students who need to change the way they think about tests. You may see these students have some of the same feelings you have. You will learn how each of these kids faced their problems and ended up doing better on tests.

Stay-Away Stephanie

Stephanie thought that it was better to stay away from tests than to try at all. She was scared to face tests. She thought, "If I stay home sick, I won't have to take the test. I don't care if I get in trouble, I'm just not going to take the test." Stay-Away Stephanie felt less nervous when she ran away from tests, but she never learned to face her fear. Stephanie's teacher thought Stephanie didn't care about tests or school, but this wasn't true at all. Stay-Away Stephanie really worried about tests. She stayed away instead of trying to face each challenge.

One day, Stephanie's mom had an idea! "Stephanie, do you remember when you were afraid to ride your bike when I took the training wheels off?" her mom asked. "You would hide whenever I wanted to take a bike ride. You said, 'I would rather walk than learn to ride a two-wheel bike.'" Stephanie knew that wasn't true. She did want to learn to ride the bike, but she was scared. She stayed away from the challenge. When Stephanie faced her fear, step by step, she learned to ride her bike. "Stephanie," her mom said, "I think you stay away from tests because you're worried." Stephanie knew her mom was right. She had to face tests step by step.

Stephanie and her teacher came up with a plan. First, Stephanie's teacher gave her two test questions to do in school. For homework, Stephanie did two more questions. When Stephanie was scared, she talked with her mom or her teacher. She didn't stay away. Soon, Stephanie knew how to ask for help, and she took tests without being worried. Now, she has a new nickname; it's "Super Successful Stephanie!"

If you are like Stay-Away Stephanie, talk with your teacher or someone who can help you. Together, you can learn to take tests one step at a time. You will be a super successful student instead of a stay-away student.

Worried Wendy

Wendy always thought that the worst would happen. Her mind worried about everything. "What if I can't answer all the questions? What if I don't do well? My teacher won't like me. My dad will be upset. I will have to study a lot more." Wendy spent her time worrying. Instead, she should learn to do well on tests.

Wendy was so worried her stomach hurt. Wendy's doctor knew she wasn't sick, she was worried. "Wendy," he said, "I have known you ever since you were born. You have always been curious. You wanted to know how everything worked and where everything was. But now, your curious mind is playing tricks on you. You are so worried, you're making yourself sick."

Wendy's doctor put a clock on his desk. "Look at this clock. Is it a good clock or a bad clock?" Wendy had no answer. "Believe it or not, Wendy, we can trick our mind into thinking it is good or it is bad. I'm going to say as many bad things about this clock as fast as I can. First, it's not very big. Also, because the clock is small, I might not read the time on it correctly. Since the clock is so small, I might lose it forever." Wendy agreed it was a bad clock. "But wait," said her doctor, "I think the clock is a neat shape, and I like the colors. I like having it in my office; it tells time well. It didn't cost much, so if I lose it, it isn't a big deal." Wendy realized she could look at tests the way the doctor looked at the clock. We don't have to worry. We can see good things, not bad.

Critical Carlos

Carlos always put himself down. He thought he failed at everything he did. If he got a B+ on his homework, he would say, "I made so many mistakes, I didn't get an A." He never said good things like, "I worked hard. I'm proud of my B+." Carlos didn't do well on tests because he told himself, "I don't do well on anything, especially tests."

Last week, Carlos got a 95% on a test about lakes and rivers. Carlos stared at his paper. He was upset. "What is the matter, Carlos?" His teacher asked, "Is something wrong?" Carlos replied, "I'm stupid, I missed five points. I should have gotten a 100%."

"Carlos, nobody's perfect: not me, not you, not anybody. I think 95 out of 100 is super! It's not perfect, but it is very good. Celebrate, Carlos!" Carlos smiled; he knew his teacher was right. Now Carlos knows he has to feel good about what he does. He isn't sad about his mistakes. He's cheerful, not critical.

Look at the chart below. Use this chart to find out all the good things about yourself. Some examples are given to get you started.

Good Things About Me

1. *I make my grandmother happy when I tell her a joke.*

2. *I taught my dog how to shake hands.*

3. *I can do two somersaults in a row.*

4.

5.

6.

Victim Vince

Vince couldn't take responsibility for himself. He said everything is someone else's fault. "Florida's state assessment is too hard. I won't do well because they made the test too hard. And last night, my little brother made so much noise, I couldn't write my story. It's his fault I won't do well. I asked mom to buy my favorite snack. I have to have it when I study. She forgot to pick it up at the store. I can't study without my snack. It's her fault." Vince complained and complained.

Vince's aunt told him he had to stop blaming everyone for his troubles. "You can make a difference Vince," she said. "When is your next test?" Vince told her he had a spelling test on Friday. "You're going to be the boss of the test. First, let's pick a time to study. How about 4:30 p.m. everyday?" Vince agreed. "Now, how are you going to study?"

"I like to practice writing the words a couple of times. Then, I ask mom or dad to quiz me."

"Great idea. Everyday at 4:30 p.m., you're going to write each word four times. Then, ask one of your parents to review your list. You're the boss of the spelling test Vince because you have a plan."

When Friday came, Vince's whole world changed. Instead of his bad mood and poor grade, Vince felt powerful! He took his spelling test and scored an A–. Vince could not believe his eyes! His teacher was thrilled. Vince soon learned he could control his attitude. Vince is no longer a victim. Instead, he is "Victor Vince."

Vince's Study Plan

TIME	Monday	Tuesday	Wednesday	Thursday	Friday
					Spelling Test!
4:00	Write down spelling words. Then, ask Mom or Dad to help.	Write down spelling words. Then, ask Mom or Dad to help.	Write down spelling words. Then, ask Mom or Dad to help.	Write down spelling words. Then, ask Mom or Dad to help.	
4:30					
5:00					
5:30					
6:00					
7:00	Look at spelling words again.	Look at spelling words again.	Look at spelling words again.	Look at spelling words again.	
7:30					Get a movie for doing well!

Perfect Pat

Pat spent all her time studying. She told herself, "I **should** study more. I **should** write this book report over. I **should** study every minute for Florida's state assessment." Trying hard is fine, but Pat worked so much, she never felt she had done enough. Pat always thought she should be studying. Pat would play with her friends, but she never had a good time. In the middle of kickball or crafts, Pat thought, "I should be studying for Florida's state assessment. I should be writing my book report." When Pat took a test, she worried about each question. "I can't answer this one, I should have studied harder."

"Pat," her principal said, "you have to relax. You're not enjoying school." Pat replied, "I can't do that. There is so much more to learn." The principal gave Pat some tips on how to use her study time better.

- Do not study for long periods of time. Instead, try to work for about 10–20 minutes at a time, and then take a break. Everyone needs a break!

- Ask yourself questions as you go along. After you study a fact, test yourself to see if you remember it. As you read, ask yourself questions about what you are reading. Think about what you are studying!

- Find a special time to study. You may want to think of a good time to study with the help of your parents or teacher. You could choose to study from 4:30 to 5:00 every day after school. After dinner, you could work from 7:30 to 8:00. After you finish studying, do not worry! You have done a lot for a third grader.

- Remember, you are a third-grade kid! School is very important, but playing, having fun, and being with your friends and family is also a very important part of growing up. Having fun does not mean you won't do well in school. It doesn't mean you will do poorly on Florida's state assessment. Having fun in your life makes you a happier person and helps you do better on tests.

"Everyone Else is Better" Edward

Edward worries about everyone else. During holidays, Edward thinks about the presents other people receive. At his baseball game, he worries his teammates will score more runs. Edward always wants to know how his friends do on tests. He spends so much time worrying about what other people are doing, he forgets to pay attention to his own studying.

"Edward, you're not going to succeed if you don't worry about yourself," his grandfather told him. "You need to start talking about what **you** can do. Instead of asking your friend how he did on a test, say, 'I got an 85%. Next time, I want to get a 90%.' " When Edward practiced this, he worried less about tests and was a whole lot happier.

Shaky Sam

Sam was great at sports. He was friendly and funny, and he had many friends. However, Sam had one big problem. Every time he even thought about taking a test, he would start shaking inside. His heart would start pounding like a drum. His stomach would get upset. The night before a test, he started shaking really hard.

Sam's older brother liked to sing. He told Sam he used to get nervous before he sang to a crowd of people. "Sam, we need to trick your body. Don't think about the test, think about something fun and happy."

Sam closed his eyes. He thought about making four shots in a row on the basketball court. He thought about his favorite dessert—vanilla ice cream. He thought about swimming at his neighbor's pool. When he opened his eyes, he wasn't shaking.

Practice thinking happy thoughts, and make believe you are far away from your troubles. Test stress will disappear.

Other Ways That Third Graders Have Stopped Worrying About Tests

Third graders are pretty smart kids. They have a lot of good ideas on getting rid of test stress. This list gives tips on how to stop worrying.

- When I am scared or worried, I talk to my neighbor. She is 70 years old. She is the smartest person I know. We sit on her porch and eat cookies and talk. It makes me feel better to know she had some of the same problems. She did well in school, and I know I can do it, too.

- Everything is harder in third grade, especially reading and math. I didn't want to go to school. I talked to my teacher, and he said, everyday before class we should have a talk. We talk about my homework, and he gives me tips. This really calms me down. When I am calm, I always do better.

- I used to worry that I wasn't doing well in school. I thought everyone else was smarter. My dad gave me a special folder. I keep all my tests in it. When I look at the tests, I see how much I have learned. I know I am doing a good job.

Florida kids are smart kids! You, your teachers, and your family and friends can help you find other ways to beat test stress. You will be surprised how much you know and how well you will do on Florida's state assessment.

Test-Taking Hints for Test Heroes

Introduction

Many third graders have not yet seen a multiple-choice test, such as Florida's state assessment. Before you sit down to take the test, it is a good idea to review problem-solving and test-taking strategies. The words "test-taking strategies" may be overwhelming to third graders, so we have titled the chapter, "Test-Taking Hints for Test Heroes."

This chapter offers several hints you can use when you face Florida's state assessment as well as many other tests. The ideas will build confidence and improve test-taking techniques.

Do Your Best on Florida's State Assessment: Think Like a Genius!

Most third graders think the smartest kids do the best on tests. Smart kids may do well on tests, but all kids can do their best. By learning some helpful hints, most kids can do better than they ever thought!

Learning to do well on tests will be helpful to you throughout your whole life, not just in third grade. Kids who are "test smart" feel very good about themselves. They have an "I can do it" feeling about themselves. This feeling helps them succeed in school, in sports, in music. It even helps with making friends. Test-smart kids usually do well in their schoolwork too. They believe they can do anything!

Become an Awesome Test Hero!

1. **Fill In the Answer Bubble**

   You will use a pencil to take Florida's state assessment. Think about tests you have taken. To answer questions, you may have written an answer, circled the correct answer, or solved a math problem. Florida's state assessment is different. You will use your pencil to fill in an answer bubble. The test is multiple choice. This means you will have four choices to pick from. After you read the question and all the answer choices, think about which choice is correct. Next to each choice you will see an answer bubble. The answer bubbles are not very big. They are smaller than the end of an eraser, smaller than a dime, and smaller than a jellybean. Even though the answer bubbles are small, they are very important! To answer the question, you must fill in the answer bubble of the correct choice. Only fill in one answer bubble for each question. Fill in the bubble all the way, and do not color outside the bubble. Make sure you fill in the answer bubble neatly when you take Florida's state assessment.

Look at the example below. You can see the correct way to fill in an answer bubble. Practice filling in the answer bubbles in this example.

There was a girl named Devine,
Who thought that a dot was a line!
She didn't fill in the bubble;
She was really in trouble!
When her answers are wrong she will whine!

Correct: ● Incorrect:

Practice filling in the answer bubbles here: ○ ○ ○ ○ ○

Learning how to fill in answer bubbles takes practice, practice, and more practice! It may not be how you are used to marking the correct answer, but it is one way to give a right answer on Florida's state assessment. Think about Kay!

A stubborn girl named Kay,
Liked to answer questions her own way.
So her marked answer bubbles,
Gave her all sorts of troubles.
Her test scores ruined her day!

2. Only Fill In One Answer Bubble

It is not a good idea to touch the answer bubbles with your pencil until you are ready to fill in the right answer. If you put marks on more than one answer bubble, the people who grade your test won't know which choice you think is right. Sometimes kids get a little worried during the test. They might play with their pencils and tap their answer booklets. This is not a good idea. Look at all the answer choices. Only fill in one answer bubble. This should be the answer bubble for the choice you think is right. Do not put marks in any other answer bubbles.

There was a nice girl named Sue,
Who thought she knew what to do.
She marked all the spots.
Her paper was covered with dots!
And she didn't show all that she knew.

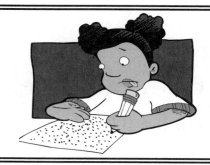

3. Think Good Thoughts

The better you feel about taking tests, the better you will do. Imagine you are a famous sports hero. You feel good about playing your favorite sport. You feel good about yourself. As a sports hero, you don't start a soccer game, football game, baseball game, tennis match, or swimming meet by saying, "This is going to be hard. I can't do it." Instead you say, "This may be a little hard, but I can do it. I am glad I have a chance to do this. I am going to do my best. I know I can." You may think Florida's state assessment is a little hard, but you can do it. When you start Florida's state assessment, remember to think good thoughts. This will help you be the best test hero you can be.

There was a girl named Gail,
Who thought she always would fail.
She said, "Tests are tough,"
"I'm not smart enough."
She had a sad end to her test-taking tale.

4. What Happens if I Don't Do Well on the Test?

Florida's state assessment is one way to find out how much you have learned by the third grade. It is important to try your best on Florida's state assessment, but remember, your friends, parents, and teachers will like you no matter how you do on this test.

> There was a nice boy named Chad,
> Who thought if he failed he was bad.
> His teacher said, "That's not true."
> "I like you no matter how you do."
> Now Chad is glad and not sad.

5. Don't Be Too Scared or Too Calm

Being too scared about tests will get in the way of doing your best. If you are scared, you won't be able to think clearly. If you are scared, your mind can't focus on the test. You think about other things. Your body might start to feel nervous. There is a chapter in this book called "Worry Less About Tests." It will help you feel calmer about tests. Read that chapter so you can feel calmer about Florida's state assessment and other tests.

If you are too calm before taking a test, you might not do well. Sometimes kids say, "I don't care about this!" They might not have pride in their schoolwork. They may be nervous. They may think Florida's state assessment is "no big deal" and may try to forget about it. If you do not think a test is important, and you try to forget about it, you are not thinking good thoughts. Don't be scared of the test, but don't forget about it. You can become a test hero and do your best if you take pride in your work.

> There was a student named Claire,
> Who usually said, "I don't care."
> Her sister named Bess,
> Always felt total stress.
> They weren't a successful pair!

6. Don't Rush, Speeding Through the Test Doesn't Help

The last time you took a test, did you look around the room to see who finished first? If someone handed his or her paper in before you, did you feel like you needed to hurry up? Kids feel that way sometimes, but rushing through questions will not help you on Florida's state assessment. Finishing Florida's state assessment first, or second, or even third is not important. This may be a surprise to learn. Usually, we think speed is good. We hear about the fastest computer, the fastest runner, and the world's fastest train. Speed is exciting to think about, but working fast on Florida's state assessment will not make your test score better. Take your time, and you will be able to show what you know!

There was a third grader named Liz,
Who sped through her test like a whiz.
She thought she should race
At a very fast pace,
But it caused her to mess up her quiz.

7. Read Directions Carefully!

One of the best ways to become a test hero is to read directions. Directions help you understand what you're supposed to do. On Florida's state assessment, it is really important to take your time and to read directions. You may say, "Why should I read directions? I know what to do." Here's a story that may change your mind.

Imagine you are a famous chef. Everyone thinks you make the best cakes in Florida! One day, a group of kings and queens come to Florida for an important visit. They ask you to bake a special cake for them. You have never baked this type of cake before. The kings and queens give you directions, but you don't read them. You think to yourself, "Who has time? I don't need directions. I know how to bake cakes." You don't read the directions and put them in a drawer. This is not a good idea. The directions tell you to bake the special cake at 250 degrees, but you bake the cake at 350 degrees! What do you get? A very crispy cake and very angry kings and queens. You should have read the directions!

Make sure you read directions slowly and repeat them to yourself. You should understand the directions before you begin the test.

There was a nice boy named Fred,
Who ignored almost all that he read.
The directions were easy,
But he said "I don't need these!"
He should have read them instead.

8. Don't Get Stuck on One Question

Some of the questions on Florida's state assessment will be easy. Other questions might be a little harder. Don't let that worry you! If there is a question you're not sure how to answer, use your pencil to put a mark by the question. Remember, mark the question, not the answer choice bubbles. Once you have marked the hard question, move to the next question. When you get to the end of the test, go back and try to answer the hard question. Once you have answered many easy questions, you might be able to answer the hard question with no problem.

If you circle a question and move on, you won't "get stuck." This is a good hint. Florida's state assessment has lots of questions, so you will be able to show what you know. If there is a question that puzzles your mind, just go back to it later.

> There was a sweet girl named Von,
> Who got stuck and just couldn't go on.
> She'd sit there and stare,
> But the answer wasn't there.
> Before she knew it, all the time was gone.

9. Use What You Know!

By the time you take Florida's state assessment, you will have been in school for four years. You went to kindergarten, first grade, second grade, and now you are in the third grade. You were taught a lot of things in school, but you learned many things in other places, too. You may have gathered information at the library, in a magazine, from TV, from your parents, and from many other places. Third graders have a lot of information in their brains!

Sometimes third graders forget how much they know. You may see a question that your teacher has not talked about. This is OK. You may have heard about it somewhere else. Take a minute to think about all you know.

Let's say you were asked the following question:

Melissa and her family go to California for a vacation. Melissa is excited about going to the beach and to an amusement park. She also really enjoys fresh orange juice. Melissa goes to a store to buy an orange juice treat. The sign says a one-liter bottle of orange juice costs $1.19. If Melissa buys the two-liter bottle, how much orange juice will she get?

Ⓐ a small glass of orange juice
Ⓑ enough orange juice to fill a bathtub
Ⓒ about as much orange juice as in a gallon of milk
Ⓓ enough orange juice to fill a swimming pool

This seems like a hard question. You don't know how much liquid is in a liter. Stop and think for minute! You have heard the word "liter" before, but where? You have seen the word "liter" on plastic soda pop bottles. When you think about the soda pop bottle, it looks about as big as a gallon of milk. Now you know the right answer! Even though you think you forgot the exact size of a liter, you used the information you did remember. You're on your way to becoming a test hero!

There was a boy named Drew,
Who forgot to use what he knew.
He had lots of knowledge.
He could have been in college,
But his correct answers were very few.

10. Luck Isn't Enough!

Have you ever had a lucky number, a lucky color, or even a lucky hat? Everyone believes in luck. A famous football player always wears the same shoes, game after game, because he thinks they give him good luck. This doesn't make any sense. Wearing old, smelly shoes doesn't help him play well. But, he believes in luck anyway. Believing in luck can be fun, but it is not going to help you do well on Florida's state assessment. The best way to do well is PRACTICE! Listening to your teacher, practicing the hints you have learned in this book, and learning every day in the third grade will help you do your best.

> There was a cool boy named Chuck,
> Who thought taking tests was just luck.
> He never prepared.
> He said, "I'm not scared."
> When his test scores appear, he should duck!

11. Recheck Your Answers

Everyone makes mistakes. Checking your work is very important. There once was a famous magician. He was very good at what he did, but he never checked his work. One night, he was getting ready for a big magic show. There were hundreds of people watching the show. The magician's wife said, "Check your pockets for everything you need." The magician didn't listen. "I've done this a million times," he said to himself. "I don't need to check my pockets." What a bad idea! When he got on stage, he reached his hand into an empty pocket—no magic tricks! Next time, he will recheck his pockets to do the best job possible!

Going back and checking your work is very important. You can read a paragraph over again if there is something that you do not understand or something you forget. In math, you can double check your answers to make sure that they make sense. You will not be wasting time if you recheck your work. It is important to show what you know, not how fast you can go. Making sure you have put down the right answer is a good idea.

A cute third grader named Kath,
Always forgot to recheck her math.
She thought she was done,
But wrote 11 instead of 1!
When her test scores come she won't laugh.

There was a quick girl named Jen,
Who read stuff once and never again.
It would have been nice,
If she reread it twice.
Her scores would have been better then!

Helpful Hints From Other Third-Grade Test Heroes!

Third graders all over the United States have good ideas about tests. Here are some of them!

- Ask yourself, "Did I answer the question that was asked?" Carefully read the question so you can give the right answer.

- Read each answer choice before filling in an answer bubble. Sometimes, you read the first choice, and it seems right. But, when you get to the fourth choice, you realize it is the correct answer. If you had stopped with the first choice, you would have answered the question incorrectly. It is important to read all four choices before answering the question.

- Remember, Florida's state assessment is not trying to trick you! Do not look for trick answers. There will always be a right answer. If the answer choices do not look right, mark the question and go back to it later.

- Don't look around the room! Don't worry about how fast your friends are working, and don't worry about how well they are doing. Only worry about yourself. If you do that, you will do better on the test.

Reading

Introduction

In the Reading section of Florida's state assessment for Grade 3, you will be asked questions to test what you have learned so far in school. These questions are based on the reading skills you have been taught in school through the third grade. The questions you will answer are not meant to confuse or trick you but are written so you have the best chance to show what you know.

The *Show What You Know® Florida! Grade 3, Student Workbook* includes a Reading Practice Tutorial that will help you practice your test-taking skills. Following the Reading Practice Tutorial is a full-length Reading Assessment.

About Florida's State Assessment in Reading for Grade 3

Reading passages in Florida's state assessment for Grade 3 will consist of approximately 40% nonfiction (informational) and 60% fiction (literary). Acceptable nonfiction texts include: science and history passages, diaries, historical documents, magazine articles, essays, biographies, autobiographies, editorials, advertisements, tables, charts, and graphs.

Acceptable fiction pieces include: short stories, excerpts, poems, historical fiction, fables, plays, and folk tales. Passages may include as many as 700 words and as few as 100. The average number of words per passage is 500.

Item Distribution and Scoring

The 3rd Grade Reading test uses only multiple-choice items.

You will select from four possible answer choices and fill in the correct answer bubble. Although multiple-choice items sometimes ask for the recall of facts, most of the sample items demand a more complex thought process. Each multiple-choice item on the assessment is scored 0 (incorrect) or 1 (correct). Each correct answer adds one point to the total assessment score.

Glossary

alliteration: Repeating the same sound at the beginning of several words in a phrase or sentence. For example, "The bees buzzed in the back of the blue barn."

adjectives: Words that describe nouns.

adverbs: Words that describe verbs.

antonyms: Words that mean the opposite (e.g., *light* is an antonym of *dark*).

audience: The people who read a written piece or hear the piece being read.

author's purpose: The reason an author writes, such as to entertain, to inform, or to persuade.

author's tone: The attitude the writer takes toward an audience, a subject, or a character. Tone is conveyed through the writer's choice of words and details. Examples of tone are *happy, sad, angry, gentle*, etc.

base word (also called root word): The central part of a word that other word parts may be attached to.

biography: A true story about a person's life.

cause: The reason for an action, feeling, or response.

character: A person or an animal in a story, play, or other literary work.

compare: To use examples to show how things are alike.

contrast: To use examples to show how things are different.

details: Many small parts which help to tell a story.

descriptive text: To create a clear picture of a person, place, thing, or idea by using vivid words.

directions: An order or instructions on how to do something or how to act.

draw conclusion: To make a decision or form an opinion after considering the facts from the text.

effect: A result of a cause.

events: Things that happen.

fact: An actual happening or truth.

fiction: A passage that is made up rather than factually true. Examples of fiction are novels and short stories.

format: The way a published piece of writing looks, including the font, legibility, spacing, margins, and white space.

generalize: To come to a broad idea or rule about something after considering particular facts.

genres: Categories of literary and informational works (e.g., biography, mystery, historical fiction, poetry).

Glossary

graphic organizer: Any illustration, chart, table, diagram, map, etc., used to help interpret information about the text.

heading: A word or group of words at the top or front of a piece of writing.

infer: To make a guess based on facts and observations.

inference: An important idea or conclusion drawn from reasoning rather than directly stated in the text.

inform: To give knowledge; to tell.

informational text (also called expository text): Text with the purpose of telling about details, facts, and information that is true (nonfiction). Informational text is found in textbooks, encyclopedias, biographies, and newspaper articles.

literary devices: Techniques used to convey an author's message or voice (e.g., figurative language, simile, metaphors, etc.).

literary text (also called narrative text): Text that describes actions or events, usually written as fiction. Examples are novels and short stories.

main idea: The main reason the passage was written; every passage has a main idea. Usually you can find the main idea in the topic sentence of the paragraph.

metaphor: A comparison between two unlike things without using the words "like" or "as." An example of a metaphor is, "My bedroom is a junkyard!"

mood: The feeling or emotion the reader gets from a piece of writing.

nonfiction: A passage of writing that tells about real people, events, and places without changing any facts. Examples of nonfiction are an autobiography, a biography, an essay, a newspaper article, a magazine article, a personal diary, and a letter.

onomatopoeia: The use of words in which the sound of the word suggests the sound associated with it. For example, buzz, hiss, splat.

opinion: What one thinks about something or somebody; an opinion is not necessarily based on facts. Feelings and experiences usually help a person form an opinion.

passage: A passage or writing that may be fiction (literary/narrative) or nonfiction (informational/expository).

persuade: To cause to do something by using reason or argument; to cause to believe something.

plan: A method of doing something that has been thought out ahead of time.

plot: A series of events that make up a story. Plot tells "what happens" in a story, novel, or narrative poem.

plot sequence: The order of events in a story.

poetry: A type of writing that uses images and patterns to express feelings.

Glossary

point of view: The way a story is told; it could be in first person, omniscient, or in third person.

predict: The ability of the reader to know or expect that something is going to happen in a text before it does.

prefix: A group of letters added to the beginning of a word. For example, <u>un</u>tie, <u>re</u>build, <u>pre</u>teen.

preposition: A word that links another word or group of words to other parts of the sentence. Examples are *in, on, of, at, by, between, outside*, etc.

problem: An issue or question in a text that needs to be answered.

published work: The final writing draft shared with the audience.

reliable: Sources used for writing that are trustworthy.

resource: A source of help or support.

rhyme: When words have the same last sound. For example, hat/cat, most/toast, ball/call.

root word (also called base word): The central part of a word that other word parts may be attached to.

schema: The accumulated knowledge that a person can draw from life experiences to help understand concepts, roles, emotions, and events.

sentence: A group of words that express a complete thought. It has a subject and a verb.

sequential order: The arrangement or ordering of information, content, or ideas (e.g., a story told in chronological order describes what happened first, then second, then third, etc.).

setting: The time and place of a story or play. The setting helps to create the mood in a story, such as inside a spooky house or inside a shopping mall during the holidays.

simile: A comparison between two unlike things, using the words "like" or "as." "Her eyes are as big as saucers" is an example of a simile.

solution: An answer to a problem.

stanzas: Lines of poetry grouped together.

story: An account of something that happened.

story elements: The important parts of the story, including characters, setting, plot, problem, and solution.

style: A way of writing that is individual to the writer, such as the writer's choice of words, phrases, and images.

suffix: A group of letters added to the end of a word. For example, teach<u>er</u>, color<u>ful</u>, sugar<u>less</u>, etc.

summary: To retell what happens in a story in a short way by telling the main ideas, not details.

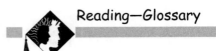

Glossary

supporting details: Statements that often follow the main idea. Supporting details give you more information about the main idea.

symbolism: Something that represents something else. For example, a dove is a symbol for peace.

synonyms: Words with the same, or almost the same, meaning (e.g., *sketch* is a synonym of *draw*).

theme: The major idea or topic that the author reveals in a literary work. A theme is usually not stated directly in the work. Instead, the reader has to think about all the details of the work and then make an inference (an educated guess) about what they all mean.

title: A name of a book, film, play, piece of music, or other work of art.

tone: A way of writing that conveys a feeling.

topic sentence: A sentence that states the main idea of the paragraph.

valid: Correct, acceptable.

verb: A word that shows action or being.

voice: To express a choice or opinion.

Reading Practice Tutorial

Directions for Taking the Reading Practice Tutorial

The Reading Practice Tutorial contains four reading passages and 14 practice questions. It should take about 30 to 45 minutes to read the passages and answer all the questions. You will mark your answers in this workbook. If you don't understand a question, just ask your teacher to explain it to you.

This section will review the Strands, Standards, and Benchmarks used to assess student achievement in the state of Florida. Following the description of each Benchmark, a sample reading passage and practice items are given. Each item gives you an idea of how the Benchmark may be assessed. Review these items to increase your familiarity with Florida-style multiple-choice questions. Once you have read through this Tutorial section, you will be ready to complete the Reading Assessment.

Tips for Taking Florida's State Assessment in Reading

Here are some hints to help you show what you know when you take the Reading Practice Tutorial and the Reading Assessment:

- Read the directions carefully. Ask your teacher to explain any directions you do not understand.

- Read the passages and questions very carefully. You may look back at a passage as often as you like.

- Answer the questions you are sure about first. If a question seems too difficult, skip it and go back to it later.

- Be sure to fill in the answer bubbles correctly. Do not make any stray marks around answer spaces.

- Think positively. Some questions may seem hard, but others will be easy.

- Check each answer to make sure it is the best answer for the question asked.

- Relax. Some people get nervous about tests. It's natural. Just do your best.

Sample Multiple-Choice Item

To help you understand how to answer the test questions, look at the sample test question below. It is included to show you what a multiple-choice question in the test is like and how to mark your answer in your workbook.

1 Why did the author MOST LIKELY include a letter written to Robert?

   Ⓐ   to help us understand why Robert wanted to visit his grandfather

   ●   to prove that Robert's grandfather was alive

   Ⓒ   to make us feel for Robert's grandfather

   Ⓓ   to tell us what he thinks about Robert's grandfather

For this sample question, the correct answer is choice B "to prove that Robert's grandfather was alive"; therefore, the circle next to choice B is filled in.

Reading Practice Tutorial

Read the poem "Clouds" before answering Numbers 1 through 3.

Look up at the clouds
And what do you see?
I see a man's face
Looking back at me.
He has two big eyes,
A nose, and an ear.
I wonder now
If clouds need to hear.
Gray but glowing
Like the man on the moon.
I know it's not him.
It's just after noon.
Puffy like pillows
Clouds creep on their own,
Sneaking away slowly
To places unknown.
But then the cloud changes
As I watch from below.
The face fades away
And leaves only a glow.

Now answer Numbers 1 through 3. Base your answers on the poem "Clouds."

1 Read this sentence from the poem.

   The face fades away.

When the face *fades*, it

   Ⓐ   slowly disappears.

   Ⓑ   gets bigger.

   Ⓒ   moves in circles.

   Ⓓ   changes color.

2 Read these lines from the poem.

   Sneaking away slowly
   To places unknown.

Which word has the same base word as *slowly*?

   Ⓕ   slopped

   Ⓖ   stopping

   Ⓗ   slotted

   Ⓘ   slowness

3 Read this line from the poem.

Sneaking away slowly

Which word has the OPPOSITE meaning of the word *sneaking*?

Ⓐ wondering

Ⓑ cheating

Ⓒ slipping

Ⓓ showing

Read the article "Marsupials" before answering Numbers 4 through 9.

What are Marsupials?

The word marsupial means "pouched animal." Marsupials are mammals. They are warm-blooded animals. They are born live, and they drink their mothers' milk. There is something special about marsupials: they have a pouch. The female marsupial's pouch is a built-in nursery. Soon after its birth, a baby marsupial finds its way to its mother's pouch. A baby marsupial will live and grow in the pouch for several months.

Most marsupials live in Australia. Australia is a continent in the South Pacific Ocean. There are about 200 types of marsupials in the world. Types of marsupials include kangaroos, koalas, wombats, Tasmanian devils, wallabies, and opossums. The opossum is the only marsupial that lives in North America.

KANGAROOS

Facts about Kangaroos

Kangaroos usually come to mind when people think of pouched animals. There are many types of kangaroos, including the red, the rat, and the gray. Kangaroos grow to many sizes. Some are only one foot tall, but others grow to be six feet high. Kangaroos never run. Their back legs would get in the way if they tried. Instead, kangaroos use their long, strong back legs to help them jump up to three or four times their body's length. They also push off the ground with their tails as they begin a jump. Although kangaroos can jump at speeds of up to 30 miles per hour, they can only hop at this speed for very short distances.

Kangaroos live in groups called mobs. A mob may include 100 kangaroos. If you want to see a kangaroo, your best chance would be at night or very early in the morning when they are most active. During the middle of the day, they try to stay cool under trees or bushes. They live in many different settings (places) including grasslands, hills, or woodlands. Kangaroos like to graze on grass and other small plants.

Kangaroo Babies

Baby kangaroos weigh about one ounce at birth. They are about the size of a lima bean. They are blind at birth and have no fur. A baby kangaroo lives in its mother's pouch for about five months. Baby kangaroos are called joeys, but they are also known as "young-at-foot." Kangaroos usually give birth to only one baby at the time, but kangaroo mothers with "twins" have been spotted.

Facts about Koalas

The koala looks like a teddy bear, but it is not a bear at all. In fact, koalas may be more like monkeys. They live in trees, and they use their strong claws to hold on to branches in eucalyptus trees.

Koalas must live in thick eucalyptus forests, because adults need to eat between one and two pounds of the leaves daily. Koalas rarely drink water. They get the water they need from the leaves of the eucalyptus tree. The word "koala" actually means "no drink."

Baby Koalas

Koalas are one of the types of marsupials whose pouches open to the rear of their bodies. A baby koala lives in its mother's pouch for seven months. Then, the baby moves to the mother's back and lives in this "piggyback" position for five more months.

Now answer Numbers 4 through 10. Base your answers on the article "Marsupials."

4 Read this sentence from the article.

They are born live, and they drink their mothers' milk.

Which sentence uses the word *live* the same as it is used in the sentence above?

- Ⓕ The girls live in a log cabin.
- Ⓖ The tadpoles turned into live frogs.
- Ⓗ The concert was presented live.
- Ⓘ My brother and I live two miles from our aunt.

5 Why did the author MOST LIKELY write the article "Marsupials"?

- Ⓐ to show how kangaroos live
- Ⓑ to describe how baby kangaroos and baby koalas live and grow
- Ⓒ to inform about marsupials
- Ⓓ to show how marsupials are born

6 What happens AFTER the baby koala lives in its mother's pouch for seven months?

  Ⓕ The baby begins to graze on grass and other small plants.

  Ⓖ The baby drinks water and eats eucalyptus.

  Ⓗ The baby moves to the mother's back.

  Ⓘ The baby lives in the grasslands, hills, or woodlands.

7 Your best chance to see a kangaroo is at night or very early in the morning because

  Ⓐ it is cooler at those times.

  Ⓑ they live in grasslands and hills.

  Ⓒ they jump very quickly.

  Ⓓ they live in their mothers' pouches.

8 What information can be found under the heading "What are Marsupials?"

  Ⓕ the reason marsupials live in Australia

  Ⓖ a comparison of kangaroos and koalas

  Ⓗ a definition of a marsupial

  Ⓘ the steps to feeding a marsupial

9 What topic is covered in this article?

Ⓐ mammals

Ⓑ kangaroos

Ⓒ pouched animals

Ⓓ koalas

10 Read the sentence from the article "Marsupials."

The female marsupial's pouch is a built-in nursery.

What is the author comparing the pouch to in the above sentence?

Ⓕ a human baby's room

Ⓖ a human baby's blanket

Ⓗ an adult marsupial's resting place in the bushes

Ⓘ an adult marsupial's fur

Read the story "The Kitchen" before answering Numbers 11 through 12.

My favorite room in the house is the kitchen. I love to eat, so that's my number one reason. But there are other reasons, too. I love the yummy smells that come from the oven when a cake or cookies are baking. I love the way the kitchen sounds: bacon sizzling in a frying pan, or the kettle whistling on the stove. I love squishing ground beef in my fingers and forming the perfect size hamburger. I love to see foods changing shape as they cook on the stove or in the oven. And the tastes! Just think of juicy lemons, oatmeal cookies, cheesy pizza, warm biscuits, crisp apples, and fresh tomatoes. My list of favorites goes on and on. I think I'll head to the kitchen now. For some reason, my stomach is growling.

Now answer Numbers 11 through 13. Base your answers on the story "The Kitchen."

11 Which word BEST describes the narrator in the story?

Ⓐ hungry

Ⓑ lazy

Ⓒ warm

Ⓓ fun

12 Read this sentence from the story.

> **I love the way the kitchen sounds: bacon sizzling in the frying pan, or the kettle whistling on the stove.**

What mood does the author create by writing that bacon is *sizzling* and the kettle is *whistling*?

Ⓕ exciting

Ⓖ scary

Ⓗ boring

Ⓘ smelly

13 Which sentence from the story BEST describes what is happening in the illustration on page 36?

Ⓐ My favorite room in the house is the kitchen.

Ⓑ I love the yummy smells that come from the oven when a cake or cookies are baking.

Ⓒ I love the way the kitchen sounds: bacon sizzling in a frying pan, or the kettle whistling on the stove.

Ⓓ I love squishing ground beef in my fingers and forming the perfect size hamburgers.

Read the story "Georgia" before answering Number 14.

Georgia

James Oglethorpe founded Georgia as a colony in 1733. A colony is made up of a group of people who live together in a certain area. Georgia was named in honor of King George II of Great Britain. The first city in Georgia was Savannah. It was settled the same year the colony was formed. In 1788, Georgia became the fourth state in the United States of America. At that time, Georgia's population was around 60,000 people. Today, Georgia is home to more than 8 million people. Georgia is often called "The Peach State." Its capital city is Atlanta.

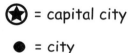
⊛ = capital city
● = city

Now answer Number 14. Base your answer on the story "Georgia."

14 What does the ★ symbol mean on the map?

    ⓕ   city

    ⓖ   north

    ⓗ   west

    ⓘ   capital city

This is the end of the Reading Practice Tutorial.
Until time is called, go back and check your work or answer questions
you did not complete. When you have finished, close your workbook.

This page left intentionally blank.

Reading Assessment

Directions for Taking the Reading Assessment

The Reading Assessment contains eight reading passages and 45 questions. Some of the passages are fiction, while others are nonfiction. Read each passage and the questions that follow carefully. You may look back at any passage as many times as you would like. If you are unsure of a question, you can move to the next question, and go back to the question you skipped later.

This test contains multiple-choice questions. Multiple-choice questions require you to pick the best answer out of four possible choices. Only one answer is correct. Remember to read the questions and the answer choices carefully. You will mark your answers in this workbook. Fill in the answer bubble to mark your selection.

Reading Assessment

Read the article "A Symbol of Pride" and look over the fact box "The America Flag" before answering Numbers 1 though 6.

An important patriotic symbol of the United States is our national flag. Our flag represents the land, the people, and the government of the United States. On June 14, 1777, the Continental Congress declared (said) the flag of the United States would have thirteen stripes. The stripes would alternate red and white. This means one stripe would be red, the next stripe would be white; then, the next stripe would be red, and so on. The Continental Congress also said the flag would have a union (group) of thirteen white stars on a blue background. The thirteen stripes represented the thirteen original colonies. These thirteen colonies were the first states in the United States. The thirteen stars represented the number of states in the United States, at that time.

The Continental Congress did not say how the stars should be arranged on the blue background, so flag makers used different designs. Sometimes, twelve stars were placed in a circle on the blue background with one star in the middle of the circle. Other times, the thirteen stars were placed in a circle on the blue background.

As new states became part of the United States, more stars and stripes were added to the flag. After awhile, people thought the flag had too many stripes. The Flag Act of 1818 stated the design of the American flag would include only thirteen stripes. The stripes were for the thirteen original colonies. The Flag Act also said the American flag should have one white star for each state that joins the United States. In 1846, the flag had 29 stars. By 1861, the number of stars had grown to 34, and in 1898, the flag contained 45 stars. The last change to the flag was in 1960 when a star was added for the state of Hawaii. On July 4 of that year, President Dwight D. Eisenhower approved the final arrangement of the 50 stars. The design of this 50-star flag is the one we still use today.

The American flag has had several nicknames over the years. Our country's earliest flag was known as the Continental flag or the Congress colors. Today, it is sometimes called the Stars and Stripes, Old Glory, or the Red, White, and Blue. No matter what name is used, the flag we see flying today is an important symbol of pride for our country.

The American Flag

These are some examples of the American Flag. As you can see, there have been many different designs of the American Flag. Throughout the history of the United States, there have been more than 25 different designs. Here are just three examples.

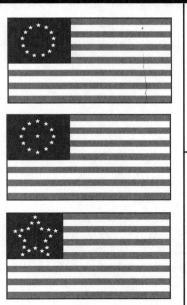

This is the current American Flag. The United States has used this design since 1960. The 50 stars represent our country's 50 states.

color key

■ = blue

■ = red

□ = white

Even though the American flag has had many designs, the colors have always been the same. Our flag includes red stripes, white stripes, white stars, and a blue square.

Now answer Numbers 1 through 6. Base your answers on the article "A Symbol of Pride" and the fact box "The American Flag."

1 Read this sentence from the article.

> **The Continental Congress did not say how the stars should be arranged on the blue background, so flag makers used different designs.**

Which word has the SAME meaning as the word *arranged*?

Ⓐ makers

Ⓑ say

Ⓒ placed

Ⓓ moved

2 In what year did President Eisenhower approve the design of the current American flag?

Ⓕ 1777

Ⓖ 1861

Ⓗ 1960

Ⓘ 1898

3 Based on "The American Flag" section, how many stripes does the current American flag have?

Ⓐ 14

Ⓑ 13

Ⓒ 7

Ⓓ 50

4 How are the flag of 1818 and the current American flag ALIKE?

   Ⓕ   The stars on both flags represent the original colonies.

   Ⓖ   The stripes on both flags represent cities in the United States.

   Ⓗ   The colors used on both flags are the same.

   Ⓘ   The colors used on both flags are red, white, and green.

5 Why did the author MOST LIKELY write the article "A Symbol of Pride"?

   Ⓐ   to tell about the history of the American flag

   Ⓑ   to tell about President Dwight Eisenhower

   Ⓒ   to explain the Flag Act of 1818

   Ⓓ   to describe how to take care of a flag

6 Who said the original flag of the United States would have thirteen stripes?

   Ⓕ   President Eisenhower designed the flag with thirteen stripes.

   Ⓖ   The Flag Act of 1818 said the flag should have thirteen stripes.

   Ⓗ   The citizens of the United States voted to include thirteen stripes on the flag.

   Ⓘ   The Continental Congress said the flag would have thirteen stripes.

Read the story "Good Morning, Sunshine" before answering Numbers 7 through 12.

Good Morning, Sunshine!

Annie woke up to a ray of sunlight on her face. She blinked her eyes and stretched her arms out from beneath her blankets. She couldn't believe it was morning already. It seemed as if she had just gone to sleep. Staring at the ceiling, she thought about her day and remembered what was going to happen in just two hours. Annie's stomach began to churn. She sat up, but fell back onto her pillow. She closed her eyes again, secretly wishing it would all be over.

Her mother knocked and opened the bedroom door just a crack. She saw that Annie was awake. "Good morning, Sunshine. It's time to get up! You don't want to waste a second this morning."

But that's exactly what Annie wanted to do. Slowly, Annie pulled herself out of bed and looked around the room that was now hers. It was still a mess. Moving boxes were everywhere. Four white, empty walls stared back at her. Maybe it would be better when things were unpacked. That's what her mom and dad kept telling her. Annie couldn't believe it would ever feel as comfortable as her old room.

The light of the sun made it possible to study each wall; it had been too dark the night before. One wall had a tiny crack that looked a little like a spider. "I'll never like a room with a spider crack," she thought to herself. Her mind was made up.

A pair of jeans, a purple shirt, and some sneakers—all brand new—were piled in the corner. Annie's mother surprised her daughter with the gift just yesterday. Annie knew her mother was trying to make her feel better, but Annie thought she might be more comfortable in her old clothes. New clothes never felt as good to her as her old ones. Since Annie didn't even know where to start looking for her old favorites, she settled for the new attire.

"Annie, I don't hear you moving. Are you up, Sunshine?"

"Why does she always call me that?" wondered Annie. It was a nickname Annie didn't like, but she had grown used to it. "She should call me 'Grumpy,'" Annie whispered to herself. "That's how I feel." With her shoes tied and her hair combed, she traveled into the unfamiliar hallway and down the stairs to greet a plate of pancakes.

"Oh, Annie, you look great!" her mom smiled as she poured a tall glass of milk.

"Thanks," Annie said, but she didn't really mean it. Around and around, she pushed syrup-soaked flapjacks around her plate. "How can I eat?" she thought. "My insides are tied in knots." Annie watched the clock count down the remaining moments of summer.

"Let's go, Annie." Her dad's voiced echoed. "You're going to miss the bus."

Now answer Numbers 7 through 12. Base your answers on the story "Good Morning, Sunshine."

7 What happens AFTER Annie looks for her old clothes but BEFORE she goes downstairs?

Ⓐ Annie's stomach begins to churn.

Ⓑ Annie settles for the new clothes.

Ⓒ Annie finds a crack on the wall.

Ⓓ Annie watches the clock.

8 Why does Annie feel like her stomach is tied in knots?

Ⓕ She is nervous about her first day at a new school.

Ⓖ She doesn't like what she was going to have for breakfast.

Ⓗ She has to wear her old clothes to school instead of the new ones.

Ⓘ She doesn't feel well.

9 Which word BEST describes Annie in this story?

Ⓐ happy

Ⓑ lonely

Ⓒ grumpy

Ⓓ jolly

10 What is Annie's MAIN problem in the story?

(F)   She hasn't cleaned her room for two weeks.

(G)   She packed up all her things because she wants to paint the walls.

(H)   Her little brother made a mess the night before.

(I)   She and her family just moved into a new house.

11 How is Annie's new room DIFFERENT from her old room?

(A)   Annie's new room is more comfortable.

(B)   Annie's old room was a different color.

(C)   Annie's old room was bigger.

(D)   Annie's new room has a spider crack.

12 Read the sentence from the story "Good Morning, Sunshine."

Annie's stomach began to churn.

What is the author comparing Annie's stomach to in the above sentence?

(F)   a spider hiding in her room

(G)   a machine in which butter is made

(H)   the pancakes that her mother is cooking

(I)   milk that has gone sour

Read the article "The Olympic Games" before answering Numbers 13 through 18.

The Olympic Games

Today, the Olympic Games include some of the most popular sporting events in the world. Many of the events we see in today's Olympics are based on games from ancient Greece—games played over two thousand years ago. Believe it or not, many of the sports we watch today also took place a long time ago. ✓

The first Olympic Games were held thousands of years ago. People would travel for many miles to gather for the five-day festival. The Games began with an opening ceremony. Visitors would watch men compete in footraces, wrestling, horse and chariot races, and the pentathlon. The pentathlon was a combination of five events. Athletes ran, jumped, threw a discus, threw a javelin, and wrestled. Only men were allowed to take part in the ancient Olympics. The Olympics were held every fours years in the summer. Only summer sports were part of the ancient Games. Winners were given a crown made of leaves. The events of the original Olympic Games were stopped about 1,600 years ago, around the year 393.

The first modern Olympic Games were held in 1896. These Games took place in Athens, Greece. About 300 athletes competed (played) in the Games. Only summer events were included. The tradition of the Olympic Games has continued. The Summer Olympic Games include some of the same events as the ancient games. Athletes throw the discus and javelin, run in races of different lengths, and wrestle. The modern Olympics have many more sports. These include swimming, diving, tennis, volleyball, and many more.

The modern Olympic Games are different from the ancient Olympics in other ways, too. The Games now offer more than summer sports. The first Winter Olympics were held in 1924. Some Winter Olympic sports are skiing, skating, hockey, and basketball. The Summer and Winter Games still begin with an opening ceremony, but each is held in a different city every four years. Also, the Olympic athletes of today include both men and women. Another difference: winners receive medals in gold for first place, silver for second place, and bronze for third place finishes.

While many things have changed, the Olympic Games continue to be an event where people watch their favorite athletes compete to be the best in their events. It is a time when people come together to cheer, to compete, and to show pride in their abilities and in their countries.

Now answer Numbers 13 through 18. Base your answers on the article "The Olympic Games."

13 Read this sentence from the article.

> **Many of the events we see in today's Olympics are based on games from ancient Greece.**

Ancient Greece means that the games came from

Ⓐ   long ago

Ⓑ   yesterday

Ⓒ   modern times

Ⓓ   four years ago

14 How are the ancient Olympics and the modern Olympics ALIKE?

Ⓕ   Both included men and women.

Ⓖ   Both had races, volleyball, and tennis.

Ⓗ   Both included summer and winter sports.

Ⓘ   Both awarded prizes to winners.

15 Why did the author MOST LIKELY write the article "The Olympic Games"?

Ⓐ   to inform the reader about the first Olympic Games in Greece

Ⓑ   to tell about the summer and winter Olympic Games

Ⓒ   to explain when the Olympic Games became popular in Greece and around the world

Ⓓ   to explain how the modern Olympics and the ancient Olympics are alike and different

16 What topic is covered in this article?

    Ⓕ   events played in the Olympic games

    Ⓖ   modern Olympic games and ancient Olympic games

    Ⓗ   winners of the Olympic games

    Ⓘ   prizes from the Olympic games

17 Read these sentences from the article.

> **The pentathlon was a combination of five events. Athletes ran, jumped, threw a discus, threw a javelin, and wrestled.**

When an athlete competes in a *pentathlon*, they are competing in

    Ⓐ   the opening ceremonies for the Olympic games.

    Ⓑ   the race to win the gold, silver, or bronze medals.

    Ⓒ   five running and throwing events in the summer Olympics.

    Ⓓ   a game played by women in ancient Greece.

18 The modern Olympics are DIFFERENT from the ancient Olympics because

    Ⓕ   the ancient Olympics included winter sports.

    Ⓖ   the modern Olympics include winter sports.

    Ⓗ   the modern Olympics do not honor winners.

    Ⓘ   the ancient Olympics included women.

Read the story "Tony's Skunk" before answering Numbers 19 through 23.

Tony's Skunk

Tony had never been so scared. The light of his flashlight was fixed on a small animal. The bright eyes of a skunk stared at him. "You're smaller than my puppy," he whispered. He knew the animal wouldn't attack him. Yet, he was afraid to move a muscle. "What am I going to do?" he thought. Tony knew if he did the wrong thing, he would be very sorry.

This was the first time Tony had spotted a skunk. Tony didn't know much about the black and white creature, but he knew he must be careful. When skunks are scared, they spray a liquid that smells very bad. This liquid, which comes from a gland near the base of the tail, keeps predators away. Tony knew the skunk would growl and stomp its feet if it was about to spray. So, he carefully watched the little animal.

The skunk seemed startled. "He's as scared as I am," Tony thought. Tony's eyes were locked on the skunk. The skunk's eyes were fixed on Tony. A few more moments passed. Tony was ready to make a decision. "I hope I'm doing the right thing."

Tony began to move away slowly. He never let his eyes leave the skunk. He picked up his right foot, then his left. He softly whispered to himself, "I don't want to hurt you. Just let me get away from you."

The skunk was motionless. Tony moved away from him. Inch by inch, Tony backed away through the brush. He didn't want to move his flashlight off the skunk. He couldn't see where he was walking. He hoped he didn't stumble and fall. The leaves softly crunched under his feet. The skunk remained motionless.

He started to feel a bit of relief. Tony was about twelve feet from the little animal. He continued to step gently. Then suddenly, his foot came down and "CRACK!" The sound echoed about. It was only a dry stick, but it made Tony jump. The flashlight hit the ground. Light bounced around the brush. Tony's heart was beating fast. He couldn't see the skunk. The light no longer hit the skunk's eyes. Tony heard a small growl. "Oh no! I'm going to get it!" But Tony was lucky; the skunk had different plans. Tony heard four small footsteps running through the brush. Relieved, Tony scooped up his flashlight and quickly headed in the opposite direction.

Now answer Numbers 19 through 23. Base your answers on the story "Tony's Skunk."

19 Why was Tony scared?

Ⓐ He thought the skunk might bite him.

Ⓑ The light on his flashlight did not work.

Ⓒ He thought the skunk might spray him.

Ⓓ He was lost in the woods.

20 What happened AFTER Tony steps on the dry stick but BEFORE he hears a growl?

Ⓕ Tony sees the skunk.

Ⓖ Tony drops his flashlight.

Ⓗ The skunk sprays Tony.

Ⓘ Tony's foot hurt.

21 Read these sentences from the story.

Light bounced around the brush. Tony's heart was beating fast.

What mood does the author create by writing that Tony's heart was *beating fast*?

Ⓐ scary

Ⓑ calm

Ⓒ funny

Ⓓ sad

© Englefield & Associates, Inc.

22 How does Tony try to solve his problem with the skunk?

    Ⓕ He throws his flashlight at the skunk.

    Ⓖ He growls at the skunk to scare it.

    Ⓗ He slowly steps away from the skunk.

    Ⓘ He cracks a stick to scare the skunk.

23 When Tony first steps away from the skunk, he is unable to see where he is walking because

    Ⓐ he dropped his flashlight.

    Ⓑ his flashlight does not have batteries.

    Ⓒ Tony forgot his flashlight at home.

    Ⓓ the flashlight is pointed at the skunk.

Read the story "Carrots and Gravy" before answering Numbers 24 through 30.

There are two foods I never want to see on my plate: carrots and gravy. I don't mean together. I dislike them separately. For as long as I can remember, I have never liked these two. I'm not sure why. Mom says, even when I was little, carrots and gravy weren't for me.

We have a special rule in our house. At dinner, we have to try everything on our plates. I've tried carrots with salad and gravy with potatoes, but nothing works. I'm nine years old, and I still don't like carrots or gravy. I know I never will. A few weeks ago, carrots were served, again. I complained, but mom just looked at me. I knew the rule. I swallowed the orange mess. I grabbed my throat. I grabbed by belly. I fell from my chair. Mom just looked at me.

"I guess he's tried long enough. If Julio survives, no more carrots. I promise."

I lifted my head off the floor. "What about gravy?" I smiled.

"We'll see."

Mom kept her promise, and all was going great until a special family dinner. Mom and I met my grandparents at their favorite restaurant. We were celebrating their wedding anniversary. My uncle and his son Jake were there, too. Jake is a year older; he's in fourth grade. Jake and I both wanted hamburgers and french fries with lots of ketchup. We sat at the table, practicing our orders. A waitress came by and served a few glasses of water.

"Your dinners will be ready, soon."

"But we haven't ordered, yet." Jake and I were confused.

"It's been taken care of," she said. "I just know you're going to love it."

My uncle had called ahead to save time. I was disappointed. I was really looking forward to my hamburger. The waitress was right. Our dinner started in no time at all. The salad came first, but it was piled with little carrot slices. I tried to be polite. I pushed the orange pieces to the side of my plate. When my salad was free of carrots, I enjoyed every last bite. "This isn't so bad," I thought.

After taking away our salad plates, it was time for the main course. "Please!" I whispered to Jake, "let it be something I like!" I held my breath. The plate was in front of me. I peeked. Turkey and mashed potatoes covered in gravy! Mom smiled at me. I didn't grab my throat or my belly. Instead, I shrugged my shoulder and gave her half a smile. I spent most of the dinner just moving things around on my plate. Everyone was busy talking. No one seemed to notice.

"Are you going to eat that?" Jake asked. I shook my head no. He heaped the dinner onto his plate. "This stuff is great." I couldn't believe he thought so. All that gravy—yuck.

I thought my mom would be mad, but on our way home, she stopped at Happy Burger. I didn't even ask her to. "What will you have, Julio?" Mom asked.

"I'll take a cheeseburger and fries. No carrots. No gravy."

Now answer Numbers 24 through 30. Base your answers on the story "Carrots and Gravy."

24 Why did Julio's mom stop at Happy Burger?

- Ⓕ She had a coupon for free french fries.

- Ⓖ She knew Julio didn't eat much at the restaurant.

- Ⓗ She was hungry.

- Ⓘ She took Julio to Happy Burger to celebrate his birthday.

25 What is Julio's MAIN problem in the story?

- Ⓐ He didn't like the restaurant he was going to with his family.

- Ⓑ He grabbed his throat and his belly and fell to the floor.

- Ⓒ He was served food he didn't like at the restaurant.

- Ⓓ He was bored so he pushed his food around his plate.

26 How are Julio and Jake ALIKE?

- Ⓕ They both wanted to order hamburgers.

- Ⓗ They both enjoyed the dinner at the restaurant.

- Ⓗ They are the same age.

- Ⓘ They both go to the same school.

27 Read this sentence from the story.

He heaped the dinner onto his plate.

When Jake *heaped* Julio's dinner onto his plate, he

(A)   threw Julio's dinner at him.

(B)   piled Julio's dinner on his plate.

(C)   ate Julio's dinner.

(D)   stole Julio's dinner plate.

28 What is the FIRST thing served at the restaurant?

(F)   turkey and mashed potatoes with gravy

(G)   salads with carrots on top

(H)   glasses of water

(I)   hamburgers and french fries

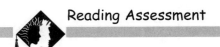

29 Why did the author MOST LIKELY write the story "Carrots and Gravy"?

   Ⓐ   to convince readers to try all foods on their plates

   Ⓑ   to tell a story about Julio, a boy who doesn't like carrots or gravy

   Ⓒ   to explain why people should eat at Happy Burger instead of at nice restaurants

   Ⓓ   to describe why Julio has to eat carrots and gravy

30 How do you know Julio's mom is not mad at him when he doesn't eat his dinner at the restaurant?

   Ⓕ   She fixes him a hamburger when they get home from the restaurant.

   Ⓖ   She lets him eat dessert, even though he didn't finish the main course.

   Ⓗ   She tells him she is not mad at him.

   Ⓘ   She stops at Happy Burger to get him some food.

Read the article "Journal Writing" before answering Numbers 31 through 37.

Writing in a journal is a great way to keep track of things in your life. A journal can also be called a diary. Writers use journals to record their thoughts and ideas. Some people use journals to collect story ideas. Others write about bad days or happy times. Keeping a journal can help you reflect or think about what is happening in your life. When you read what you have written in your journal, you can learn from your everyday experiences.

It doesn't take any fancy materials to start a journal. You can start with a simple notebook and a pen or a pencil. You can get a special notebook if you want to make your journal more fancy. You can also use a computer to start your journal. The important thing is to record your thoughts and ideas. You can write them on paper or you can type them, whichever way is the best for you.

Try to write in your journal every day. You don't need to write for a long period of time, maybe only five or ten minutes, at first. As you keep practicing, you may find that you want to write for a few more minutes.

Writing a journal is a good way to practice your writing skills. Even though your journal is filled with your own words, try to use your best handwriting (if you're writing in a notebook). You want to be able to read what you have written! Also, try to spell words correctly and use complete sentences. Working on these skills will help you become a better writer.

Another secret to journal writing is to keep track of your writing. Put the date on each piece. This will help you remember when things happened. Every week or so, go back and read what you have written. You might find that something that seemed important has been forgotten. You might also find words that surprise you. Whatever the case, keep writing. You may be surprised at how much you have to say.

Journal Ideas

Write about things that happen each day.

Write about books you have read.

Keep a dialogue journal.
You and another person (a friend, parent, or teacher) write back and forth to each other.

Write stories.

Write about something new you learn each day.

Journal Materials

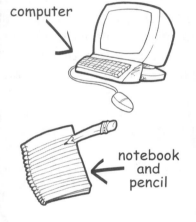

computer

notebook and pencil

Important Things to Remember

Write every day.

June 9, 2010
Write the date on each piece.

Review what you have written.

Practice good writing skills.

Now answer Numbers 31 through 37. Base your answers on the article "Journal Writing."

31 Under which heading would you MOST LIKELY find information about items needed for journal writing?

    Ⓐ   Journal Writing

    Ⓑ   Journal Ideas

    Ⓒ   Journal Materials

    Ⓓ   Important Things to Remember

32 What is the topic covered in this article?

    Ⓕ   keeping a journal

    Ⓖ   ideas to write in a journal

    Ⓗ   things to remember in a journal

    Ⓘ   choosing a type of journal

33 Based on the article, how often does this author think you should write in your journal under the "Journal Writing" section?

    Ⓐ   once a week

    Ⓑ   twice a day

    Ⓒ   once a day

    Ⓓ   once an hour

34 Read the sentence from the article " Journal Writing."

> **Another secret to journal writing is to keep track of your writing.**

A *secret* is

(F)   something to tell everyone.

(G)   something to make open to all.

(H)   something that is kept unknown.

(I)   something to only tell a few people.

35 Read this sentence from the article.

> **This will help you remember when things happened.**

Which word has the OPPOSITE meaning of the word *remember*?

(A)   think about

(B)   review

(C)   forget

(D)   recall

36 With which statement would the author of this article MOST LIKELY agree?

  Ⓕ A journal is only for you, so spelling and neatness are not important.

  Ⓖ You want to be able to read what you have written.

  Ⓗ You should not write too much in your journal.

  Ⓘ A journal needs to be fancy.

37 At the beginning of the article, what does the author say you can learn from reading what you have written in your journal?

  Ⓐ You can learn how to write in a journal.

  Ⓑ You can learn new journal ideas.

  Ⓒ You can learn new words and phrases.

  Ⓓ You can learn from your everyday experiences.

Read the story "The Key" before answering Numbers 38 through 43.

THE KEY

Emma noticed a small, white box on the stairs. She picked it up carefully and opened it to find a small key wrapped in a lace handkerchief. Faded pink and blue flowers decorated the delicate handkerchief, and the initials "A.B." were stitched into one corner. Emma assumed that it could belong to her grandmother because her name, Abby Brown, matched the initials.

As Emma examined the key, she saw that it was a dull, golden color. It was about as long as her index finger and seemed heavy for its size. There was a bit of crumpled blue ribbon looped through the hole at the top of the key. Emma thought to herself that the key must be very old because it was so worn. Emma wanted to find her grandmother and ask her about the key. As she went from room to room looking for her grandmother, Emma imagined that there might be wonderful treasures somewhere for that key to unlock. Then, Emma remembered that Gramma had gone to the store. Emma's questions would have to wait until she returned.

Emma was sitting on the porch step when Gramma returned. She slowly removed the key from her pocket and held it up for Gramma to see. "Look what I found—is it yours?" Emma asked. A broad smile appeared on Gramma's face as she inspected the key. "I thought I had lost this," Gramma said. "This key opens a very special box I have stored in the attic." Then, Gramma took Emma's hand and said, "Come with me. I have something to show you."

Emma and her grandmother walked through the house to the back stairs that led up to the attic. As they climbed the steep steps to the storage place, Emma's mind raced with thoughts about that special box. She pondered what it would look like and, most importantly, what would be inside the box.

Now answer Numbers 38 through 43. Base your answers on the story "The Key."

38 Where was Emma waiting when her grandmother returned?

    Ⓕ   inside the house

    Ⓖ   in the backyard

    Ⓗ   on the porch

    Ⓘ   in the car

39 Which pair of words from the story has almost the SAME meaning?

    Ⓐ   decorated, delicate

    Ⓒ   returned, examined

    Ⓒ   pondered, thought

    Ⓓ   crumpled, imagined

40 What event happens AFTER Emma finds the key but BEFORE her grandmother returns home?

    Ⓕ   Emma finds the old key.

    Ⓖ   Emma finds a small white box.

    Ⓗ   Emma imagines that she would find treasure.

    Ⓘ   Emma shows her grandmother the key that she found.

41 Read this sentence from the story.

As Emma examined the key, she saw that it was a dull, golden color.

Which word has the same base word as *golden*?

Ⓐ goodness

Ⓑ glider

Ⓒ goldenly

Ⓓ glossy

42 What is the setting in the story?

Ⓕ Emma's Gramma's house

Ⓖ Emma's house

Ⓗ Emma's Gramma's attic

Ⓘ Emma's Gramma's backyard

43 How are Emma and Gramma ALIKE?

Ⓐ Both Emma and Gramma are nervous about what is inside of the special box.

Ⓑ Both Emma and Gramma are excited about what is inside of the special box.

Ⓒ Both Emma and Gramma are scared about what is inside of the special box.

Ⓓ Both Emma and Gramma do not care about what is inside of the special box.

Read the story "The Upset Storm" before answering Numbers 44 through 45.

The Upset Storm

I had waited for this day for weeks. The day of our big field trip had arrived, finally, the fun trip. This wasn't a trip to a museum or a play. We weren't going to listen to someone talk about desert plants. This trip was about having fun. My classmates and I would soon be riding water slides and splashing in the big pool's blue waters. I couldn't wait.

Mom packed my lunch. My juice box was at the bottom of the bag. My sandwich and chips were on the top so they wouldn't get smashed. I knew what I wanted to wear. I put my new T-shirt, my swimsuit, and a big towel on a chair in my room. I set two alarm clocks. I didn't want to oversleep. I wanted everything to be perfect.

Before I went to sleep, I watched the TV weatherman. He said a big storm was coming. I changed the channel. I hoped a new weather report would be different. It was not. A big storm would arrive the next morning, the morning of our big day, the day of the fun trip.

I thought about the trip. I couldn't sleep. Up in my room, I hoped for better weather. But I knew the storm was going to upset our plans. I couldn't believe it. A storm! Instead of splashing in the pool, I would be sitting at my desk, working on math problems. How could the weather do this to me?

Now answer Numbers 44 through 45. Base your answers on the story "The Upset Storm."

44 Why does the narrator set two alarm clocks?

    (F)   She is afraid she will oversleep.

    (G)   She is worried about the storm.

    (H)   She is excited about the storm.

    (I)   She is excited about the field trip.

45 What is the MAIN idea of the story?

    (A)   It is a lot of work getting ready for a field trip.

    (B)   The weather is unpredictable.

    (C)   Most field trips are boring.

    (D)   The weather is going to ruin a great field trip.

> ## This is the end of the Reading Assessment.
> Until time is called, go back and check your work or answer questions
> you did not complete. When you have finished, close your workbook.

Mathematics

Introduction

In the Mathematics section of Florida's state assessment, you will be asked questions designed to test what you have learned in school. These questions have been written based on the mathematics you have been taught in school through third grade. The questions you answer are not meant to confuse or to trick you but are written so you have the best opportunity to show what you know about mathematics.

The *Show What You Know® Florida! Grade 3, Student Workbook*, includes a Mathematics Practice Tutorial that will help you practice your test-taking skills. Following the Mathematics Practice Tutorial is a full-length Mathematics Assessment.

About Florida's State Assessment in Mathematics for Grade 3

Items in this section of Florida's state assessment will test your ability to perform mathematical tasks in real-world and mathematical situations, and will neither require you to define mathematical terminology nor memorize specific facts. Florida's state assessment is meant to gauge your ability to apply mathematical concepts to a given situation. This will include the addition, subtraction, multiplication, and division of whole numbers; addition and subtraction of decimals; addition and subtraction of simple fractions; and measurement. Items are written so that you will not need a calculator. A ruler is provided for use with certain questions.

The Assessment will contain 45 Mathematics questions and you will be given 120 minutes to complete the Assessment.

Item Distribution and Scoring

Florida's state assessment for 3rd Grade Mathematics uses only multiple-choice items.

You will select from four possible answer choices and fill in a bubble in your answer book. Although multiple-choice items sometimes ask for the recall of facts, most of the sample items demand a more complex thought process. Each multiple-choice item on the Assessment is scored 0 (incorrect) or 1 (correct). Each correct answer adds one point to the total assessment score.

Glossary

addend: Numbers added together to give a sum. For example, 2 + 7 = 9. The numbers 2 and 7 are addends.

addition: An operation joining two or more sets where the result is the whole.

a.m.: The hours from midnight to noon; from Latin words *ante meridiem* meaning "before noon."

analyze: To break down information into parts so that it may be more easily understood.

angle: A figure formed by two rays that meet at the same end point called a vertex. Angles can be obtuse, acute, right, or straight.

area: The number of square units needed to cover a region. The most common abbreviation for area is *A*.

Associative Property of Addition: The grouping of addends can be changed and the sum will be the same. Example: (3 + 1) + 2 = 6; 3 + (1 + 2) = 6.

Associative Property of Multiplication: The grouping of factors can be changed and the product will be the same. Example: (3 x 2) x 4 = 24; 3 x (2 x 4) = 24.

attribute: A characteristic or distinctive feature.

average: A number found by adding two or more quantities together and then dividing the sum by the number of quantities. For example, in the set {9, 5, 3}, the average is 6: 9 + 5 + 4 = 18; 18 ÷ 3 = 6. *See mean.*

axes: Plural of axis. Perpendicular lines used as reference lines in a coordinate system or graph; traditionally, the horizontal axis (*x*-axis) represents the independent variable and the vertical axis (*y*-axis) represents the dependent variable.

bar graph: A graph using bars to show data.

capacity: The amount an object holds when filled.

chart: A way to show information, such as in a graph or table.

circle: A closed, curved line made up of points that are all the same distance from a point inside called the center. Example: A circle with center point *P* is shown below.

circle graph: Sometimes called a pie chart; a way of representing data that shows the fractional part or percentage of an overall set as an appropriately sized wedge of a circle. Example:

■ blue
□ green
▨ red
■ yellow

circumference: The boundary line or perimeter of a circle; also, the length of the perimeter of a circle. Example:

Commutative Property of Addition: Numbers can be added in any order and the sum will be the same. Example: 3 + 4 = 4 + 3.

Commutative Property of Multiplication: Numbers can be multiplied in any order and the product will be the same. Example: 3 x 6 = 6 x 3.

compare: To look for similarities and differences. For example, is one number greater than, less than, or equal to another number?

conclusion: A statement that follows logically from other facts.

Glossary

cone: A solid figure with a circle as its base and a curved surface that meets at a point.

cones

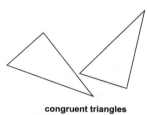

congruent figures: Figures that have the same shape and size.

congruent triangles

cube: A solid figure with six faces that are congruent (equal) squares.

cylinder: A solid figure with two circular bases that are congruent (equal) and parallel to each other connected by a curved lateral surface.

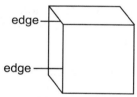

data: Information that is collected.

decimal number: A number expressed in base 10, such as 39.356, where each digit's value is determined by multiplying it by some power of 10.

denominator: The bottom number in a fraction.

diagram: A drawing that represents a mathematical situation.

difference: The answer when subtracting two numbers.

distance: The amount of space between two points.

dividend: A number in a division problem that is divided. Dividend ÷ divisor = quotient. Example: In 15 ÷ 3 = 5, 15 is the dividend.

$$\text{divisor}\overline{)\text{dividend}}^{\text{quotient}} \qquad 3\overline{)15}^{\,5}$$

divisible: Can be divided by another number without leaving a remainder. Example: 12 is divisible by 3 because 12 ÷ 3 is an integer, namely 4.

division: An operation that tells how many equal groups there are or how many are in each group.

divisor: The number by which another number is divided. Example: In 15 ÷ 3 = 5, 3 is the divisor.

$$\text{divisor}\overline{)\text{dividend}}^{\text{quotient}} \qquad 3\overline{)15}^{\,5}$$

edge: The line segment where two faces of a solid figure meet.

equality: Two or more sets of values that are equal.

equation: A number sentence that says two expressions are equal (=). Example: 4 + 8 = 6 + 6.

equivalent fractions: Two fractions with equal values.

estimate: To find an approximate value or measurement of something without exact calculation.

even number: A whole number that has a 0, 2, 4, 6, or 8 in the ones place. A number that is a multiple of 2. Examples: 0, 4, and 678 are even numbers.

expanded form: A number written as the sum of the values of its digits. Example: 546 = 500 + 40 + 6.

Glossary

expression: A combination of variables, numbers, and symbols that represent a mathematical relationship.

face: The sides of a solid figure. For example, a cube has six faces that are all squares. The pyramid below has five faces—four triangles and one square.

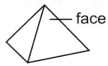
face

fact family: A group of related facts using the same numbers. Example: 5 + 8 = 13; 13 − 8 = 5.

factor: One of two or more numbers that are multiplied together to give a product. Example: In 3 x 4 = 12, 3 and 4 are factors of 12.

figure: A geometric figure is a set of points and/or lines in 2 or 3 dimensions.

flip (reflection): The change in a position of a figure that is the result of picking it up and turning it over. Example: Reversing a "b" to a "d."
Tipping a "p" to a "b" or a "b" to a "p" as shown below:

fraction: A symbol, such as $\frac{2}{8}$ or $\frac{5}{3}$, used to name a part of a whole, a part of a set, or a location on the number line. Examples:

$$\frac{numerator}{denominator} = \frac{dividend}{divisor}$$

$$\frac{\text{\# of parts under consideration}}{\text{\# of parts in a set}}$$

function machine: Applies a function rule to a set of numbers, which determines a corresponding set of numbers.
Example: Input 9 ➞ Rule x 7 ➞ Output 63. If you apply the function rule "multiply by 7" to the values 5, 7, and 9, the corresponding values are:

$$5 \rightarrow 35$$
$$7 \rightarrow 49$$
$$9 \rightarrow 63$$

graph: A "picture" showing how certain facts are related to each other or how they compare to one another. Some examples of types of graphs are line graphs, pie charts, bar graphs, scatterplots, and pictographs.

grid: A pattern of regularly spaced horizontal and vertical lines on a plane that can be used to locate points and graph equations.

hexagon: A six-sided polygon. The total measure of the angles within a hexagon is 720°.

regular hexagon   irregular hexagons

impossible event: An event that can never happen.

integer: Any number, positive or negative, that is a whole number distance away from zero on a number line, in addition to zero. Specifically, an integer is any number in the set {. . .-3,-2,-1, 0, 1, 2, 3. . .}. Examples of integers include: 1, 5, 273, -2, -35, and -1,375.

intersecting lines: Lines that cross at a point. Examples:

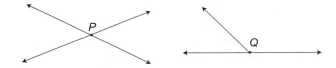

Glossary

isosceles triangle: A triangle with at least two sides the same length.

justify: To prove or show to be true or valid using logic and/or evidence.

key: An explanation of what each symbol represents in a pictograph.

kilometer (km): A metric unit of length: 1 kilometer = 1,000 meters.

line: A straight path of points that goes on forever in both directions.

line graph: A graph that uses a line or a curve to show how data changes over time.

line of symmetry: A line on which a figure can be folded into two parts so that the parts match exactly.

liter (L): A metric unit of capacity: 1 liter = 1,000 milliliters.

mass: The amount of matter an object has.

mean: Also called arithmetic average. A number found by adding two or more quantities together, and then dividing the sum by the number of quantities. For example, in the set {9, 5, 3} the mean is 6: 9 + 5 + 4 = 18; 18 ÷ 3 = 6. *See average.*

median: The middle number when numbers are put in order from least to greatest or from greatest to least. For example, in the set of numbers 6, 7, 8, 9, 10, the number 8 is the median (middle) number.

meter (m): A metric unit of length: 1 meter = 100 centimeters.

method: A systematic way of accomplishing a task.

mixed number: A number consisting of a whole number and a fraction. Example: $6\frac{2}{3}$.

mode: The number or numbers that occur most often in a set of data. Example: The mode of {1, 3, 4, 5, 5, 7, 9} is 5.

multiple: A product of a number and any other whole number. Examples: {2, 4, 6, 8, 10, 12,…} are multiples of 2.

multiplication: An operation on two numbers that tells how many in all. The first number is the number of sets and the second number tells how many in each set.

number line: A line that shows numbers in order using a scale. Equal intervals are marked and usually labeled on the number line.

number sentence: An expression of a relationship between quantities as an equation or an inequality. Examples: 7 + 7 = 8 + 6; 13 < 92; 56 + 4 > 59.

numerator: The top number in a fraction.

octagon: An eight-sided polygon. The total measure of the angles within an octagon is 1080º.

regular   irregular
octagon   octagons

odd number: A whole number that has 1, 3, 5, 7, or 9 in the ones place. An odd number is not divisible by 2. Examples: The numbers 53 and 701 are odd numbers.

operation: A mathematical process that combines numbers; basic operations of arithmetic include addition, subtraction, multiplication, and division.

order: To arrange numbers from the least to greatest or from the greatest to least.

Glossary

ordered pair: Two numbers inside a set of parentheses separated by a comma that are used to name a point on a coordinate grid.

parallel lines: Lines in the same plane that never intersect.

parallelogram: A quadrilateral in which opposite sides are parallel.

pattern: An arrangement of numbers, pictures, etc., in an organized and predictable way. Examples: 3, 6, 9, 12, or ® 0 ® 0 ® 0.

pentagon: A five-sided polygon. The total measure of the angles within a pentagon is 540°.

regular   irregular
pentagon   pentagon

perimeter: The distance around a figure.

perpendicular lines: Two lines that intersect to form a right angle (90 degrees).

pictograph: A graph that uses pictures or symbols to represent similar data. The value of each picture is interpreted by a "key" or "legend."

Key
Each picture =
10 pieces of fruit

place value: The value given to the place a digit has in a number.
Example: In the number 135, the 1 is in the hundreds place so it represents 100 (1 x 100), the 3 is in the tens place so it represents 30 (3 x 10), and the 5 is in the ones place so it represents 5 (5 x 1).

p.m.: The hours from noon to midnight; from the Latin words *post meridiem* meaning "after noon."

point: An exact position often marked by a dot.

polygon: A closed figure made up of straight line segments.

ABCDEF is a polygon.

possible event: An event that might or might not happen.

predict: To tell what you believe may happen in the future.

prediction: A description of what may happen before it happens.

probability: The likelihood that something will happen.

product: The answer to a multiplication problem. Example: In 3 x 4 = 12, 12 is the product.

pyramid: A solid figure in which the base is a polygon and faces are triangles with a common point called a vertex.

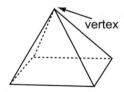

vertex

quadrilateral: A four-sided polygon. Rectangles, squares, parallelograms, rhombi, and trapezoids are all quadrilaterals. The total measure of the angles within a quadrilateral is 360°. Example: *ABCD* is a quadrilateral.

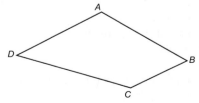

questionnaire: A set of questions for a survey.

Glossary

quotient: The answer in a division problem. Dividend ÷ divisor = quotient. Example: In 15 ÷ 3 = 5, 5 is the quotient.

range: The difference between the least number and the greatest number in a data set. For example, in the set {4, 7, 10, 12, 36, 7, 2}, the range is 34; the greatest number (36) minus the least number (2): (36 − 2 = 34).

rectangle: A quadrilateral with four right angles. A square is one example of a rectangle.

reflection: The change in the position of a figure that is the result of picking it up and turning it over. *See flip.*

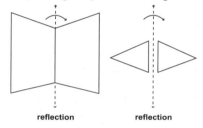

reflection   reflection

remainder: The number that is left over after dividing. Example: In 31 ÷ 7 = 4 R 3, the 3 is the remainder.

represent: To present clearly; describe; show.

rhombus: A quadrilateral with opposite sides parallel and all sides the same length. A square is one kind of rhombus.

right angle: An angle that forms a square corner and measures 90 degrees.

right triangle: A triangle having one right angle. *See angle and triangle.*

rounding: Replacing an exact number with a number that tells about how much or how many to the nearest ten, hundred, thousand, and so on. Example: 52 rounded to the nearest 10 is 50.

rule: A procedure; a prescribed method; a way of describing the relationship between two sets of numbers. Example: In the following data, the rule is to add 3:

Input	Output
3	6
5	8
9	12

ruler: A straight-edged instrument used for measuring the lengths of objects. A ruler usually measures smaller units of length, such as inches or centimeters.

scale: The numbers that show the size of the units used on a graph.

sequence: A set of numbers arranged in a special order or pattern.

set: A group made up of numbers, figures, or parts.

side: A line segment connected to other segments to form the boundary of a polygon.

side

similar: A description for figures that have the same shape.

slide (translation): The change in the position of a figure that moves up, down, or sideways. Example: scooting a book on a table.

solids: Figures in three dimensions.

solve: To find the solution to an equation or problem; finding the values of unknown variables that will make a true mathematical statement.

sphere: A solid figure in the shape of a ball. Example: a basketball is a sphere.

Glossary

square: A rectangle with congruent (equal) sides. *See rectangle.*

square number: The product of a number multiplied by itself. Example: 49 is a square number (7 x 7 = 49).

square unit: A square with sides 1 unit long, used to measure area.

standard form: A way to write a number showing only its digits. Example: 2,389.

standard units of measure: Units of measure commonly used; generally classified in the U.S. as the customary system or the metric system:

Customary System:
  Length
  1 foot (ft) = 12 inches (in)
  1 yard (yd) = 3 feet or 36 inches
  1 mile (mi) = 1,760 yards or 5,280 feet

  Weight
  16 ounces (oz) = 1 pound (lb)
  2,000 pounds = 1 ton (t)

  Capacity
  1 pint (pt) = 2 cups (c)
  1 quart (qt) = 2 pints
  1 gallon (gal) = 4 quarts

Metric System:
  Length
  1 centimeter (cm) = 10 millimeters (mm)
  1 decimeter (dm) = 10 centimeters
  1 meter (m) = 100 centimeters
  1 kilometer (km) = 1,000 meters

  Weight
  1,000 milligrams (mg) = 1 gram (g)
  1,000 grams (g) = 1 kilogram (kg)
  1,000 kilograms (kg) = 1 tonne (metric ton)

  Capacity
  1 liter (l) = 1,000 milliliters (ml)

---

strategy: A plan used in problem solving, such as looking for a pattern, drawing a diagram, working backward, etc.

subtraction: The operation that finds the difference between two numbers.

sum: The answer when adding two or more addends. Addend + Addend = Sum.

summary: A series of statements containing evidence, facts, and/or procedures that support a result.

survey: A way to collect data by asking a certain number of people the same question and recording their answers.

symmetry: A figure has line symmetry if it can be folded along a line so that both parts match exactly. A figure has radial or rotational symmetry if, after a rotation of less than 360º, it is indistinguishable from its former image.

Z unrotated   Z rotated 90º   Z rotated 180º

The letter Z has 180º radial or rotational symmetry.

table: A method of displaying data in rows and columns.

temperature: A measure of hot or cold in degrees.

translation (slide): A change in the position of a figure that moves it up, down, or sideways.

translation

Glossary

triangle: A polygon with three sides. The sum of the angles of a triangle is always equal to 180°.

turn: The change in the position of a figure that moves it around a point. Also called a rotation. Example: The hands of a clock turn around the center of the clock in a clockwise direction.

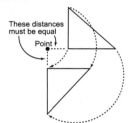

unlikely event: An event that probably will not happen.

vertex: The point where two rays meet to form an angle or where the sides of a polygon meet, or the point where 3 or more edges meet in a solid figure.

whole number: An integer in the set {0, 1, 2, 3 . . .}. In other words, a whole number is any number used when counting in addition to zero.

word forms: The number written in words. Examples: 546 is "five hundred forty-six."

Examples of Common Two-Dimensional Shapes

Right Triangle

Isosceles Triangle

Equilateral Triangle

Square

Rectangle

Parallelogram

Rhombus

Trapezoid

Pentagon

Hexagon

Octagon

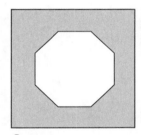
Circle

r = radius

Examples of Common Three-Dimensional Shapes

Cube

Rectangular Prism

Triangular Prism

Pyramid

Sphere

Cylinder

Cone

Examples of How Lines Interact

Acute Angle

Right Angle

Obtuse Angle

Intersecting

Perpendicular

Parallel

Lines of Symmetry

Examples of Types of Graphs

Line Graph

Double Line Graph

Pie Chart

Bar Graph

Scatterplot

Pictograph

Stem and Leaf Plot

Box and Whisker

Tree Diagram

Examples of Object Movement

Translation

Reflection

Rotation

Measurement Tools

Inch/Centimeter Rulers

This page left intentionally blank.

Mathematics Practice Tutorial

Directions for Taking the Mathematics Practice Tutorial

The Mathematics Practice Tutorial contains 16 practice questions. You will mark your answers in this workbook. It should take about 30–45 minutes to answer all the questions. If you don't understand a question, just ask your teacher to explain it to you. Calculators are NOT to be used on the Mathematics Practice Tutorial.

This section will review the Body of Knowledge, Big Idea/Supporting Idea, and Benchmarks used to assess student achievement in the state of Florida. Review these items to increase your familiarity with Florida's state assessment style multiple-choice items. Once you have completed this Tutorial section, you will be ready to complete the Mathematics Assessment.

Sample Multiple-Choice Item

To help you understand how to answer the test questions, look at the sample test question below. It is included to show you what a multiple-choice question in the test is like and how to mark your answer in your workbook.

1 Ronda has 5 stamps. Craig has 30 stamps. Which operation should be used in the box below to find how many stamps Ronda and Craig have combined?

$$5 \ \square \ 30 =$$

● addition

Ⓑ division

Ⓒ multiplication

Ⓓ subtraction

For this sample question, the correct answer is choice A "addition"; therefore, the circle next to choice A is filled in.

Mathematics Practice Tutorial

1 Mrs. Garcia can bake 9 cupcakes in one of her cupcake pans.

How many cupcakes can Mrs. Garcia bake in 3 cupcake pans?

Ⓐ   15

Ⓑ   18

Ⓒ   24

Ⓓ   27

2 Salesha is helping her mother make bridesmaid bouquets for her cousin's wedding. Yesterday, they made 6 bouquets with 8 flowers in each bouquet. Today, they made 4 more bouquets. The expression below represents the total number of flowers Salesha and her mother used.

$$(6 \times 8) + (4 \times 8)$$

Which expression below also represents the total number of flowers they used?

Ⓕ   14 + 12

Ⓖ   4 x (6 + 8)

Ⓗ   8 x (4 + 6)

Ⓘ   (6 + 8) x (4 + 8)

3 On a recent fishing trip, the Summers family caught 25 fish. Each of the 5 members of the family caught an equal number of fish. Which equation could be used to find the number of fish each member of the family caught?

Ⓐ $25 + 5 = \square$

Ⓑ $25 \times 5 = \square$

Ⓒ $\square + 5 = 25$

Ⓓ $\square \times 5 = 25$

4. William's basketball team is having a pizza party after the game. There are 8 players on the team, and three large pizzas with 8 pieces each have been ordered. Each player will get an equal amount of pizza. Which picture best represents how much pizza each player will get?

F

G

H

I

5 Ursula opened her sock drawer and saw she has a total of 15 pairs of socks in her

drawer. Of the 15 pairs of socks she has, 5 pairs are black, meaning $\frac{5}{15}$ of her sock pairs

are black, and 3 pairs are white, meaning $\frac{3}{15}$ of her sock pairs are white. The rest of her

socks are gray.

Which inequality below correctly compares the fraction of sock pairs that are black and

the fraction of sock pairs that are white?

Ⓐ $\frac{1}{3} < \frac{5}{1}$

Ⓑ $\frac{3}{1} > \frac{1}{5}$

Ⓒ $\frac{5}{1} > \frac{1}{3}$

Ⓓ $\frac{1}{3} > \frac{1}{5}$

6 Keith gave Angela a bouquet of 8 flowers for her birthday. In Angela's bouquet, $\frac{4}{8}$ of the flowers were white.

Which fraction is equal to $\frac{4}{8}$?

Ⓕ $\frac{3}{8}$

Ⓖ $\frac{1}{2}$

Ⓗ $\frac{1}{3}$

Ⓘ $\frac{4}{4}$

7 Which of following describes the figure below?

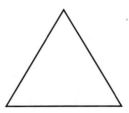

Ⓐ   square

Ⓑ   pentagon

Ⓒ   triangle

Ⓓ   rhombus

8 Roman has two shapes, as shown below.

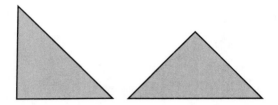

Which of following figures can Roman make by combining the shapes, without overlapping?

9 Which picture shows a line of symmetry?

Ⓐ

Ⓑ

Ⓒ

Ⓓ

10 Tim bought some small cans of soda pop. He read that each can contains 8 ounces of soda.

Soda Pop Chart

Number of Cans	Number of Ounces
1	8
2	16
3	24
4	32

If Tim bought 6 cans of soda, how many ounces of soda did he buy?

(F)   40 ounces

(G)   48 ounces

(H)   50 ounces

(I)   58 ounces

11 Max plans on putting a fence around his garden, as shown below.

6 meters

Max's Garden

5 meters

What is the perimeter of the garden?

(A)   16 meters

(B)   22 meters

(C)   23 meters

(D)   30 meters

12 Mr. Duvall had a paperclip like the one shown below.

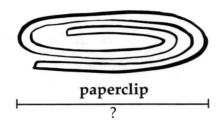

paperclip
?

Using the provided ruler, what is the exact length, in inches, of the paperclip?

Ⓕ   2 inches

Ⓖ $1\frac{1}{2}$ inches

Ⓗ $1\frac{1}{4}$ inches

Ⓘ $\frac{1}{2}$ inch

13 Carrie set her alarm clock for 7:30 a.m. Which of the clocks below shows the time 7:30?

Ⓐ

Ⓑ

Ⓒ

Ⓓ

14 Yoshi was selling shirts at the fair. He had 2,781 shirts to sell. The total number of shirts sold was between 2,000 and 2,400. What is a reasonable number of shirts that Yoshi would have left over at the end of the fair?

    (F)   200 shirts

    (G)   500 shirts

    (H)   900 shirts

    (I)   1,000 shirts

15 Augie has 5 toy trucks he likes to play with. He is only allowed to play with 2 of the trucks at a time. One of the trucks is red, 1 of the trucks is yellow, and 3 of the trucks are white.

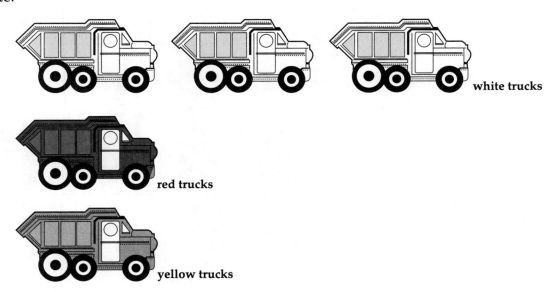

white trucks

red trucks

yellow trucks

How many different pairs of trucks would have at least 1 red truck?

Ⓐ   10 pairs

Ⓑ   5 pairs

Ⓒ   4 pairs

Ⓓ   3 pairs

16 Steve and his friends were having a juggling competition. The graph below represents the number of balls each of them was able to juggle at one time.

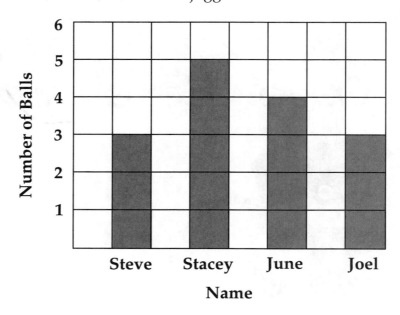

Who was able to juggle the most balls at one time?

Ⓕ   Steve

Ⓖ   Stacey

Ⓗ   June

Ⓘ   Joel

This is the end of the Mathematics Tutorial.

Until time is called, go back and check your work or answer questions you did not complete. When you have finished, close your workbook.

Mathematics Assessment

Directions for Taking the Mathematics Assessment

This Assessment test contains 45 multiple-choice questions. Multiple-choice questions require you to pick the best answer out of four possible choices. Only one answer is correct. Remember to read the questions and the answer choices carefully. You will mark your answers in this workbook. Fill in the answer bubble to mark your selection. If you do not know an answer, you may skip the question and come back to it later.

Calculators are NOT to be used on the Mathematics Assessment.

Mathematics Assessment

1 Drew is choosing a snack to have after school. He is allowed to have 1 cookie and a glass of juice. In the cookie jar, he finds 1 chocolate chip cookie and 1 oatmeal cookie. In the refrigerator, he sees 1 bottle of orange juice and 1 carton of apple juice.

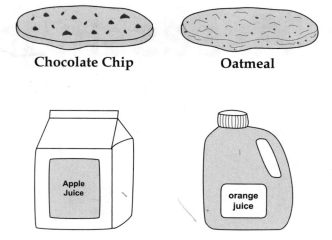

Chocolate Chip   **Oatmeal**

How many different cookie and juice combinations does Drew have to choose from?

Ⓐ 2

Ⓑ 4

Ⓒ 6

Ⓓ 8

2 Randy and Lavon each have a jar of candy.

Randy's jar   **Lavon's jar**

100 pieces   **?**

If Randy's jar has 100 pieces of candy, about how many pieces of candy are in Lavon's jar?

Ⓕ   50 pieces

Ⓖ   100 pieces

Ⓗ   200 pieces

Ⓘ   500 pieces

3 Jana started a pet walking service for the summer. She walked 2 pets the first week, 4 pets the second week, and 6 pets the third week. If her business continues to increase at the same rate each week, how many pets will she be walking next week?

Ⓐ   6 pets

Ⓑ   8 pets

Ⓒ   10 pets

Ⓓ   12 pets

4 What fraction of the rectangle below is shaded?

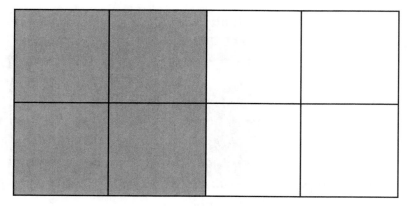

Ⓕ $\frac{1}{4}$

Ⓖ $\frac{1}{2}$

Ⓗ $\frac{4}{5}$

Ⓘ $\frac{1}{8}$

5 Which of the following best describes the figure pictured below?

Ⓐ   triangle

Ⓑ   parallelogram

Ⓒ   pentagon

Ⓓ.   square

6 Zack sketched 3 pictures a day for 5 days on his drawing pad. Which number sentence shows the correct way to find the total number of pictures Zack sketched over 5 days?

Ⓕ $3 + 5$

Ⓖ 3×5

Ⓗ $5 - 3$

Ⓘ $5 \div 3$

7 The 3 children in the Smith family must wash all the windows in their house. There are 18 windows. Mrs. Smith wants each child to wash an equal number of windows. Which equation could be used to find the number of windows each child will wash?

Ⓐ $18 + 3 = \square$

Ⓑ $18 \times 3 = \square$

Ⓒ $\square + 3 = 18$

Ⓓ $\square \times 3 = 18$

8 Mr. Oonagi's class took a field trip to a local berry farm. The farmer told the class each berry was used for making something depending on the size of the berry, as shown in the table below.

Use	Berry Size
Juice	0-2 ounces
Jam	2-4 ounces
Preserves	4-5 ounces
Canning	5+ ounces

If the farmer wants to make jam, which berry size should he use?

Ⓕ   1 ounce

Ⓖ   3 ounces

Ⓗ   4.5 ounces

Ⓘ   6 ounces

9 For the board game Imaginaria, money value is based on the length of the money. The longer the money, the more it is worth. The Imaginarian money pictured below is worth $1.00.

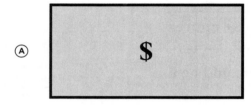

Which picture is worth $2.00?

Ⓐ

Ⓑ

Ⓒ

Ⓓ

10 The students in Mr. Sefton's class took a survey to see what holiday was most popular with the students in their class. They put their results into the graph below.

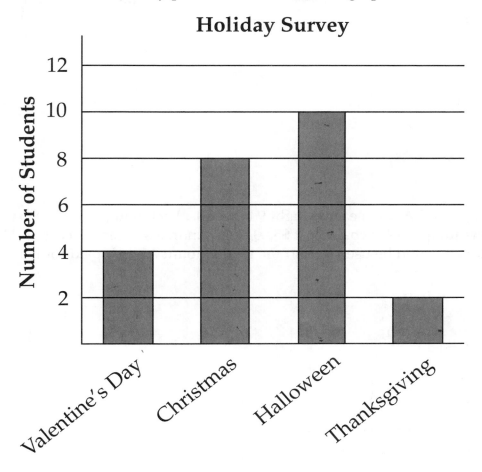

How many students are in Mr. Sefton's class?

Ⓕ   10 students

Ⓖ   12 students

Ⓗ   24 students

Ⓘ   28 students

11 The Everglades cover 1,507,850 square miles of Florida. In the figure 1,507,850, which number is in the hundreds place?

Ⓐ 0

Ⓑ 5

Ⓒ 7

Ⓓ 8

12 Juniper and Andrea each bought 9 baseballs. Each bought her baseballs at a different store. Juniper's baseballs cost $5.00 each. Andrea's baseballs cost $3.00 each. Which equation could be used to find the total amount Andrea paid for her baseballs?

Ⓕ $\square \div 9 = 3$

Ⓖ $9 + 3 = \square$

Ⓖ $9 - \square = 3$

Ⓘ $9 \div 3 = \square$

13 Carrie likes to do puzzles. The clock below shows the time Carrie finished her puzzle.

If it takes Carrie 50 minutes to do a puzzle, at what time did she start the puzzle?

Ⓐ   12:10 p.m.

Ⓑ   1:10 p.m.

Ⓒ   1:50 p.m.

Ⓓ   2:00 p.m.

14 Which figure is congruent to the figure pictured below?

Ⓕ

Ⓖ

Ⓗ

Ⓘ

15 Kim collected 8 shells while walking on the beach for 10 minutes. She collected shells for 30 minutes and then found 2 more shells on her way back home. The expression below represents the total number of shells that Kim collected in 30 minutes.

$$(8 \times 3) + 2$$

Which expression below also represents the total number of shells Kim collected?

Ⓐ $(8 \times 3) + (8 \times 2)$

Ⓑ $(8 + 2) \times (3 + 2)$

Ⓒ $2 \times (8 \times 3)$

Ⓓ $2 + (8 \times 3)$

16 There are 3 wheels on a tricycle. Which of the charts below correctly shows this information?

Ⓕ

Tricycles	Wheels
3	3
6	6
9	9

Ⓖ

Tricycles	Wheels
1	3
3	9
6	18

Ⓗ

Tricycles	Wheels
3	9
6	12
9	15

Ⓘ

Tricycles	Wheels
3	9
6	18
9	21

17 Mr. Duncan is a farmer. He has 1 chicken that lays eggs. This chicken lays 6 eggs per day. Which equation could be used to find the number of eggs laid by the chicken in 8 days?

Ⓐ $8 + 6 = \square$

Ⓑ $6 \div 8 = \square$

Ⓒ $\square \div 6 = 8$

Ⓓ $\square + 8 = 6$

18 The length of the equator is about 24,902 miles. What number is in the tens place in the figure 24,902?

Ⓕ   0

Ⓖ   2

Ⓗ   4

Ⓘ   9

19 When Allison was getting ready for school one morning, she noticed she only had 3 pairs of socks in her sock drawer. One pair of socks was white, one pair was red, and the other pair was blue.

If Allison has 2 pairs of tennis shoes to pick from, how many different combinations of pairs of socks and pairs of tennis shoes does Allison have to choose from?

Ⓐ 4

Ⓑ 5

Ⓒ 6

Ⓓ 8

20 Cindi designed the pattern shown below to put on her bicycle.

Which shape should go next to complete Cindi's pattern?

Ⓕ

Ⓖ

Ⓗ

Ⓘ

21 Mr. Hallaran made a picture frame for his photo of his dog, Samson.

Which best describes the shape of the picture frame?

(A) circle

(B) hexagon

(C) triangle

(D) square

22 Rob had 12 seeds and 3 pots to put them into. He put the same number of seeds into each pot.

Which number sentence shows how to find the number of seeds he put into each pot?

Ⓕ   12 ÷ 3

Ⓖ   12 x 3

Ⓗ   12 + 3

Ⓘ   12 − 3

23 Hector has 9 books of each of 2 different types: mystery and science fiction. He also has 4 books that are comic books. The expression below represents the total number of books that Hector has.

$$(2 \times 9) + 4$$

Which expression below also represents the total number of books Hector has?

Ⓐ   2 x (9 x 4)

Ⓑ   (2 + 4) x (9 + 4)

Ⓒ   4 + (9 x 2)

Ⓓ   9 ÷ (2 x 4)

24 Two sets of stars are pictured below. In Box A, $\frac{1}{2}$ of the stars are shaded gray. In Box B,

$\frac{3}{4}$ of the stars are shaded gray.

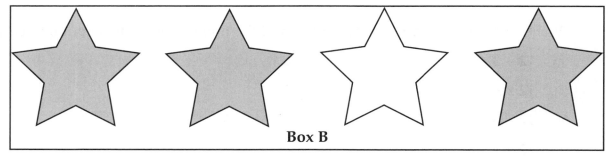

Which inequality below correctly compares the fractions of stars that are shaded gray?

Ⓕ $\frac{3}{4} < \frac{1}{2}$

Ⓖ $\frac{3}{4} > \frac{1}{2}$

Ⓗ $\frac{2}{1} < \frac{4}{3}$

Ⓘ $\frac{2}{1} > \frac{4}{3}$

25 Tim is cutting figures out of paper for a project. He needs a figure with a perimeter of 18 cm. If each of the figures shown below has line segments that are all the same length, which figure has a perimeter of 18 cm?

Ⓐ

3 cm

Ⓑ

9 cm

Ⓒ

3 cm

Ⓓ

2 cm

26 Sayid found a caterpillar like the one shown below.

Using the provided ruler, what is the exact length, **in inches**, of the caterpillar?

Ⓕ   1 inch

Ⓖ $1\frac{1}{2}$ inches

Ⓗ   2 centimeters

Ⓘ   2 inches

27 Jonathan and David are sharing a pizza that has been cut into equal-sized pieces.

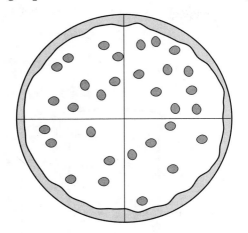

Jonathan eats some of the pizza. The picture below shows how much pizza is left.

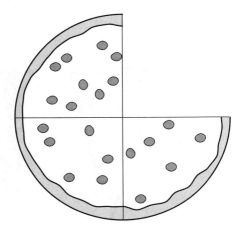

If David eats the same amount as Jonathan, how much of the pizza will be left?

Ⓐ $\frac{1}{4}$

Ⓑ $\frac{1}{3}$

Ⓒ $\frac{1}{2}$

Ⓓ $\frac{3}{4}$

28 Kendra is having ice cream cones at her birthday party. Her guests have a choice of vanilla, chocolate, or strawberry ice cream on either regular cones or sugar cones.

If guests may choose 1 kind of ice cream to go with 1 kind of cone, how many different pairs will they have to choose from?

(F) 10

(G) 8

(H) 6

(I) 4

29 Bobby drew two circles on the chalkboard for his class to compare.

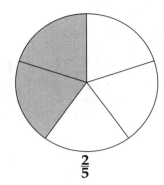

$$\frac{1}{2}$$ $$\frac{2}{5}$$

Which inequality below correctly compares the fractions of the circles that are shaded gray?

Ⓐ $\frac{1}{2} > \frac{2}{5}$

Ⓑ $\frac{1}{2} < \frac{2}{5}$

Ⓒ $\frac{1}{2} = \frac{2}{5}$

Ⓓ $\frac{1}{2} < \frac{5}{2}$

30 Eamon cut out pictures of each of the objects below. Which two pictures are congruent to each other?

31 Liza ate one piece of her chocolate chip cookie.

Liza's Cookie

Joshua's Cookie

How much of his cookie must Joshua eat to equal the amount Liza ate?

Ⓐ $\frac{2}{8}$

Ⓑ $\frac{4}{8}$

Ⓒ $\frac{6}{8}$

Ⓓ $\frac{8}{8}$

32 Which clock matches the time shown on the digital clock below?

(F)

(G)

(H)

(I)

33 Simon has two shape stickers, as shown below.

 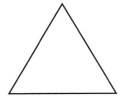

Which of these statements is false?

Ⓐ   A line can divide a rectangle into two rectangles.

Ⓑ   A line can divide a rectangle into two triangles.

Ⓒ   A line can divide a triangle into two triangles.

Ⓓ   A line can divide a triangle into two rectangles.

34 Roman's garden is in the shape of a rectangle that is 10 feet wide and 15 feet long.

15 feet

10 feet

What is the perimeter of the garden?

Ⓕ   30 feet

Ⓖ   40 feet

Ⓗ   50 feet

Ⓘ   60 feet

35 Frank wants to measure a cell phone like the one shown below.

Using the provided ruler, what is the exact length, **in inches**, of the cell phone?

Ⓐ $11\frac{1}{2}$ inches

Ⓑ 11 inches

Ⓒ $4\frac{1}{2}$ inches

Ⓓ 4 inches

36 Which figure has $\frac{5}{6}$ shaded?

Ⓕ

Ⓖ

Ⓗ

Ⓘ

37 Jamal drew the following shape on a piece of paper in his art class.

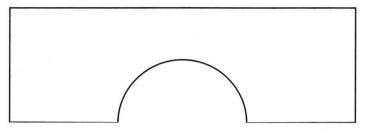

How many line segments does this figure have?

Ⓐ   4

Ⓑ   5

Ⓒ   6

Ⓓ   7

38 Devon has 7 flowerpots. She wants to plant 4 flower seeds in each pot but she lost 3 seeds when the wind blew. The expression below represents the total number of seeds that Devon has.

$$(7 \times 4) - 3$$

Which expression below also represents the total number of seeds Devon has?

Ⓕ $(4 \times 7) - 3$

Ⓖ $4 \times (7 \times 3)$

Ⓗ $(7 + 3) \times (4 + 3)$

Ⓘ $(7 - 3) \times (4 - 3)$

39 Look at the shape.

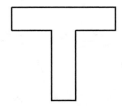

Which shape is congruent to the shape above?

(A)

(B)

(C)

(D)

40 Betty has 5 fishbowls in her house. Which picture shows fish in more than $\frac{3}{5}$ of the fishbowls?

41 Chris has a set of 12 dominoes, but noticed that $\frac{3}{12}$ of his dominoes are missing.

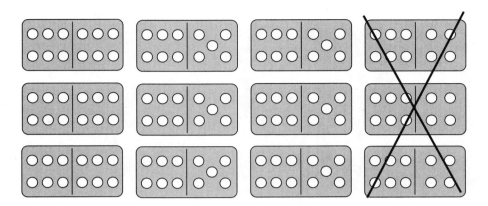

Which fraction is equal to $\frac{3}{12}$?

Ⓐ $\frac{3}{4}$

Ⓑ $\frac{1}{12}$

Ⓒ $\frac{2}{4}$

Ⓓ $\frac{1}{4}$

42 Sal has 25 fireflies and 5 jars. He will put all the fireflies in jars. If he puts the same number in each jar, how many fireflies will be in each jar?

(F) 3

(G) 4

(H) 5

(I) 6

43 Yves walked around the edge of his house. A diagram of Yves' house is shown below.

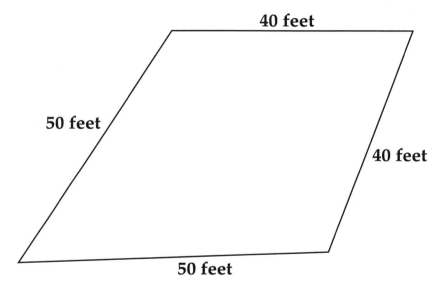

What is the perimeter of his house in feet?

(A) 160 feet

(B) 180 feet

(C) 200 feet

(D) 220 feet

44 Fritz has two foam shapes, as shown below.

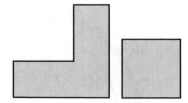

Which of the following figures can Fritz make by combining the foam shapes, without overlapping?

Ⓕ

Ⓖ

Ⓗ

Ⓘ

45 Ava went to see a movie. The clock below shows the time that Ava got to the theater.

If the movie started at 7:00, how many minutes did Ava wait at the movie theater before the movie started?

Ⓐ   30 minutes

Ⓑ   20 minutes

Ⓒ   10 minutes

Ⓓ   5 minutes

This is the end of the Mathematics Assessment.
Until time is called, go back and check your work or answer questions
you did not complete. When you have finished, close your workbook.